THE GREAT

GRAMMAR

CHALLENGE

Test yourself on punctuation, usage, grammar—and more

Publications from EEI Press

Resources for Professional Editors and Proofreaders

Mark My Words: Instruction & Practice in Proofreading

The Great Grammar Challenge: Test Yourself on Punctuation, Usage, Grammar—and More

Substance & Style: Instruction and Practice in Copyediting

Publishing: The Big Picture

Stet Again! More Tricks of the Trade for Publications People

My Big Sourcebook: For People Who Work with Words or Pictures

New York Public Library Writer's Guide to Style and Usage

Business and Marketing Resources

Letter Perfect: A Guide to Practical Proofreading

Real-World Newsletters to Meet Your Unreal Demands

Error-Free Writing: A Lifetime Guide to Flawless Business Writing

Subscription Newsletter

The Editorial Eye: Focusing on Publications Standards and Practices

THE GREAT
GRAMMAR
CHALLENGE

Test yourself on punctuation, usage, grammar—and more

Edited by Priscilla S. Taylor and Mary Stoughton

EEI PRESS®
A Division of EEI Communications

EEI Press publishes other books on editorial topics and *The Editorial Eye,* a subscription newsletter focusing on standards and practices for excellence in publications. For a free catalog, call 800-683-8380, send e-mail to press@eeicom.com, or use the Web form available at http://www.eeicom.com/press/.

EEI Press offers discounts for quantity orders from individuals, bookstores, corporations, non-profit associations, and educational organizations. For more information, call or write to

EEI PRESS®
A Division of EEI Communications

66 Canal Center Plaza, Suite 200
Alexandria, VA 22314-5507
tel 703-683-0683; fax 703-683-4915

Library of Congress Cataloging-in-Publication Data
The great grammar challenge: test yourself on punctuation, usage, grammar, and more/edited
    by Priscilla S. Taylor and Mary Stoughton.
        p.   cm.
    Compilation of "Test yourself" columns about grammar and usage from The editorial eye.
    Includes bibliographical references (p.   ) and index.
    ISBN 0-935012-21-4
    1. English language—Grammar—Problems, exercises, etc. 2. English language—
    Rhetoric—Problems, exercises, etc. 3. Report writing—Problems, exercises, etc.
    4. Editing—Problems, exercises, etc. I. Taylor, Priscilla S. II. Stoughton, Mary, 1942-   .
    III. Editorial eye.
    PE1114.G677   1997
    428'.0076—DC21   97-29858
                                                                              CIP

CONTENTS

Contents

Contents

Contents

FOREWORD AND ACKNOWLEDGMENTS

Have you had that awful, panicky dream lately? You know the one. It's the end of the semester and you're on your way to class to take a final exam when you suddenly realize that you've never gone to this particular class, you've never done any of the homework, and what's more, you don't even know where the class is being held.

Many people feel equally at a loss when they set out to improve a piece of writing. It's been a long time since they've been to class, and they still haven't done their homework! Practice may not make perfect, but it's the only way to build competence—having "good instincts" and "a feel for language" unfortunately can't take you where you need to be.

You're in good company if you've wished for a way to practice formal usage and style rules in context—that is, with problems like the ones you encounter every day instead of literary facsimiles or tortured prose. In fact, many of the examples in this book came directly from working editors and writers who turned to *The Editorial Eye,* a subscription newsletter for publications professionals, as a court of last resort. Although you may not want or need to become a grammarian, this collection of tests will help you recognize specific kinds of errors and learn how to fix them. That kind of knowledge is useful for any kind of work that involves communications skills.

These tests, which were originally published in *The Editorial Eye*, have been arranged so that they begin with the basics and move toward the finer points of careful writing and editing. They can be used as a basis for self-paced training, as the text for a formal curriculum, or as a practical adjunct to more in-depth studies of grammar.

Constructing effective test "questions" requires creativity. Finding good examples of errors, both the common ones we keep coming up against in new disguises and the uncommon ones that make us puzzle over our books, isn't easy. Even more important, a good test must have "answers" that aren't of questionable provenance or implication. *The Editorial Eye* has been devising these tests for years; more than a dozen reviewers, some of them former English teachers, have made sure that test answers were accurate and clearly reasoned and that they introduced no extraneous problems. How did these editors do this? They took the tests themselves and verified every citation.

The references that we've listed on page xiii were used as sources for the test answers; all of them are useful in their way, and we recommend that anyone with serious intentions of writing better English acquire, at a minimum, a good dictionary, an appropriate style guide, and a grammar handbook.

This book does much more than just pass along the rules of the game. A diamond-hard integrity, an insistence on correct English that comes directly from the coeditors, informs this collection. Ms. Taylor and Ms. Stoughton are from the polite but firm school of editing. By their attention to nuances of meaning and their insistence on the clearest expression of an idea, they confer integrity on any project they touch.

And integrity is what these tests are all about. Good communication requires not only consistency, which helps the reader determine meaning, but integrity, so that the language itself is equal to the task of carrying meaning. Today, when words are too often used carelessly and language sometimes seems to confuse rather than enlighten, we need standards more than ever.

This book is for people who think that splitting hairs is not only necessary but fun and who feel that writing clearly and correctly needn't be a lost cause.

—Linda B. Jorgensen
Manager, EEI Press

Acknowledgments

Over the years, many people have had a hand in making these tests; it's impossible to thank everyone. To name just a few, Eleanor Abrams, Peggy Smith, Mary Stoughton, Priscilla Taylor, and Diane Ullius devised most of these tests; Patricia Caudill, Sherrel Hissong, and Jane Rea have been debugging them for years. For this book, we did it all over again, updating style references, checking new editions of dictionaries and grammar texts, and double-checking our logic at every step. Thanks also to Patricia Caudill, Robin A. Cormier, Doreen Jones, Jayne Sutton, and Gayle Liles, who devoted hours to troubleshooting the manuscript. We couldn't have done it without you.

REFERENCES

Dictionaries and Word Guides

The American Heritage Dictionary of the English Language, 3rd Edition; Boston: Houghton Mifflin, 1992.

Merriam-Webster's Collegiate Dictionary, 10th Edition; Springfield, MA: Merriam-Webster, 1993.

Webster's Third New International Dictionary; Springfield, MA: Merriam-Webster, 1986.

Books on Grammar, Spelling, and Punctuation

The Gregg Reference Manual, 8th Edition, by William A. Sabin; Westerville, OH: Glencoe/McGraw-Hill, 1996.

Harbrace College Handbook, 13th Edition, by John C. Hodges, Winifred Bryan Horner, Suzanne Stroebeck Webb, and Robert Keith Miller; Fort Worth: Harcourt Brace College Publishers, 1998.

Style Guides

Associated Press Stylebook and Libel Manual; Reading, MA: The Associated Press, 1996.

The Chicago Manual of Style, 14th Edition; Chicago: The University of Chicago Press, 1994.

United States Government Printing Office Style Manual; Washington, DC: U.S. Government Printing Office, 1984.

Continued on next page

Books on Usage, Style, and Writing

American Usage and Style: The Consensus by Roy H. Copperud; New York: Van Nostrand Reinhold, 1980.

The Careful Writer by Theodore M. Bernstein; New York: Macmillan, 1977.

Correct Spelling Made Easy by Norman Lewis; New York: Dell, 1987.

A Dictionary of Modern English Usage by H.W. Fowler; New York: Oxford University Press, 1983.

Guidelines for Bias-Free Writing by Marilyn Schwartz and the Task Force on Bias-Free Language of the Association of American University Presses; Bloomington: Indiana University Press, 1995.

Harper Dictionary of Contemporary Usage by William and Mary Morris; New York: Harper & Row, 1985.

Modern American Usage by Wilson Follett, edited by Jacques Barzun; New York: Avenel, 1980.

The New Fowler's Modern English Usage edited by R.W. Burchfield; Oxford: Clarendon Press, 1996.

The New York Public Library Writer's Guide to Style and Usage edited by Andrea Sutcliffe; New York: HarperCollins, 1994.

Webster's Dictionary of English Usage; Springfield, MA: Merriam-Webster, 1989.

Words Into Type by Marjorie E. Skillin and Robert M. Gay; Englewood Cliffs, NJ: Prentice-Hall, 1974.

THE BASICS

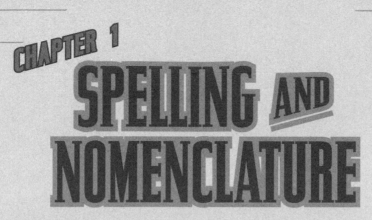

CHAPTER 1
SPELLING AND NOMENCLATURE

Nothing is more basic to good writing than spelling. Although everybody knows that some bright people are poor spellers, everybody also knows that poor spelling makes a writer appear careless or (worse) uneducated. Misspelling also distracts readers from the message.

The advent of automated spell checkers has helped. They'll save any user who takes advantage of them from *pharoah*, *grafitti*, *dessicated*, and *mocassin*, for example; but they won't help with confusables, proper names, or irregular plurals.

This chapter tests your expertise on confusing prefixes and suffixes, commonly misspelled words, assorted abbreviations, and the handling of trade names.

1-1. Judge Your Spelling Expertise

Some people seem to have been born with a special gene that makes them good spellers. The rest of us have varying degrees of trouble remembering the rules and idiosyncrasies of English spelling. To see how much you remember, answer the following questions.

1. What's the only word in the English language that ends with *-sede*?

2. What three words in the English language end with *-ceed*?

3. How do you spell the past tense of the verb *mimic*?

4. How do you spell the past tense of the verb *bus*?

5. Which spelling is correct: *judgment* or *judgement*?

6. What's the plural of each of the following *o* words? *radio, tomato, tattoo, zero, ghetto, hairdo, hero, cargo, no, alto, banjo, cello*

7. What's the plural of each of the following words ending in a *y* preceded by a vowel? *attorney, soliloquy, delay*

8. What's the plural of each of the following compound words? *forefoot, mousetrap, daughter-in-law, runner-up, deputy chief of staff, lieutenant general, court-martial, hand-me-down, notary public, attorney general, passerby*

9. What's the plural of each of the following surnames? *Crosby, Wolf, Continetti, Friedman, Fox, Jones, Matis, Bartino*

10. What's the plural of each of the following first names? *Sandi, Mary, James, Otto*

11. What's the plural of each of the following proper nouns? *Carolina, January, Allegheny* (mountains), *Rocky* (mountains)

Answers are on page 29.

1-2. *ei* or *ie*?

Fill in the blanks with ei *or* ie.

1. s__ze
2. s__ge
3. s__ve
4. b__r
5. t__r
6. m__n
7. v__n
8. v__w
9. h__ght
10. sl__gh
11. w__ght
12. w__r
13. w__rd
14. p__ce
15. n__ce
16. fr__nd
17. f__nd

18. d__gn
19. y__ld
20. for__gn
21. gr__ve
22. dec__ve
23. ach__ve
24. bel__ve
25. n__ther
26. anc__nt
27. h__nous
28. forf__t
29. l__sure
30. inv__gle
31. c__ling
32. rec__pt
33. sh__k
34. shr__k

Answers are on page 30.

1-3. The Prefix *for-* vs. *fore-*

All of the following letter groups and words start with for. *Which also need an* e *(fore)?*

1. _____bid

2. _____bode

3. _____cast

4. _____close

5. _____feit

6. _____gather

7. _____get

8. _____give

9. _____go

10. _____lorn

11. _____sworn

12. _____tell

13. _____ward

14. _____word

Answers are on page 30.

1-4. The Suffixes *-acy, -asy, -esy,* and *-isy*

Should the ending be -acy, -asy, -esy, *or* -isy?

1. advoc_____

2. apost_____

3. court_____

4. delic_____

5. diplom_____

6. ecst_____

7. effic_____

8. hypocr_____

9. idiosyncr_____

10. pleur_____

11. proflig_____

12. suprem_____

Answers are on page 31.

1-5. The Suffix *-ly* vs. *-ally*

Fill in the blanks with -ly or -ally.

1. angelic_____
2. apologetic_____
3. artistic_____
4. basic_____
5. catastrophic_____
6. climatic_____
7. clinic_____
8. cynic_____
9. diabolic_____
10. dogmatic_____
11. dramatic_____
12. eccentric_____
13. empiric_____
14. energetic_____
15. ethic_____

16. fanatic_____
17. frantic_____
18. graphic_____
19. heroic_____
20. historic_____
21. laconic_____
22. lethargic_____
23. logic_____
24. organic_____
25. prolific_____
26. public_____
27. rhythmic_____
28. specific_____
29. systematic_____
30. tragic_____

Answers are on page 31.

A Trivial Query

What do the words *ancient, deficient, science, sufficient, counterfeit, either, neither, height, seize,* and *weird* have in common? All are violations of the old rule: "Place *i* before *e*, except after *c*, or when sounded like *a*, as in *neighbor* and *weigh*."

1-6.   The Suffix *-eous* vs. *-ious*

Choose the correct spelling.

1.   a. audaceous   b. audacious

2.   a. bounteous   b. bountious

3.   a. crustatious   b. crustaceous

4.   a. disputacious   b. disputatious

5.   a. faceteous   b. facetious

6.   a. herbacious   b. herbaceous

7.   a. loquatious   b. loquacious

8.   a. ostentatious   b. ostentacious

9.   a. salacious   b. salatious

10.   a. tenatious   b. tenacious

11.   a. tendencious   b. tendentious

Answers are on page 32.

1-7. The Suffix *-or* vs. *-er*

In Correct Spelling Made Easy, *Norman Lewis says that if a root word is a verb (or comes from a verb), the spelling of the suffix for the noun is generally -er, as in* beginner, user, worker, *and* speller.

But that rule is frequently broken: Witness educator, donor, *and* inventor. *Lewis suggests that because -er is the more common ending, it's easier to just go ahead and memorize the -or words, which are more often misspelled. (The -ar suffix is even rarer, and words such as* beggar *also simply need to be memorized.)*

The problem of choosing between -or and -er is compounded because American dictionaries differ in the first spelling they give. For example, while most people recognize vendor *as correct, some dictionaries list* vender *as an alternate (that is, also correct) spelling. "One who advises" is preferably spelled* adviser, *but* advisor *is also acceptable. (The* United States Government Printing Office Style Manual, *however, restricts the use of* advisor *to "one who gives legal advice.")*

But watch out: Some words change meaning if –or is changed to -er. A sailor, *for example, is one who sails as a member of a ship's crew;* sailer, *however, refers to a ship or boat "having sailing qualities" (*Merriam-Webster's Collegiate Dictionary, *10th edition).*

If you're a bad speller, take comfort in knowing that spelling doesn't necessarily correlate with general intelligence. Keep track of the words that always trip you up by creating a personal style sheet, and use it even when you're weighing the choices your spell checker offers you.

Give the correct spelling for the following words. (One of them is correct as is.)

Noun	*Correct Spelling*
1. accelerater	_____
2. administrater	_____
3. burgler	_____
4. propeller	_____
5. elevater	_____
6. engravor	_____

Continued on next page

Noun		Correct Spelling
7.	escalater	_____
8.	fabricater	_____
9.	gossipar	_____
10.	indicater	_____
11.	investigatar	_____
12.	orater	_____
13.	transgresser	_____
14.	prisonor	_____
15.	superviser	_____
16.	Proctor & Gamble	_____

Answers are on page 32.

Spelling Trivia: *a, e, i, o, u*

Name (a) two words in which all the vowels appear in alphabetical order and (b) one word that contains all the vowels in reverse order.

b. uncomplimentary

a. abstemious and facetious, or, if you wish to count y as a vowel, abstemiously and facetiously

---

1-8. The Suffixes *-ary*, *-ery*, and *-ory*

Complete each of the following words with -ary, -ery, *or* -ory.

1. thiev_____
2. auxili_____
3. brew_____
4. distill_____
5. flatt_____
6. mock_____
7. heredit_____
8. necess_____
9. summ_____
10. cemet_____
11. diction_____
12. monast_____
13. chican_____

14. compliment_____
15. confection_____
16. document_____
17. dysent_____
18. element_____
19. exempl_____
20. fiduci_____
21. imagin_____
22. parliament_____
23. promiss_____
24. rudiment_____
25. sal_____
26. statut_____

Answers are on page 33.

1-9. The Suffixes *-able*, *-eable*, and *-ible*

Fill in the correct –able, –eable, *or* –ible *ending.*

1. challeng_____

2. chang_____

3. charg_____

4. coerc_____

5. corrig_____

6. damag_____

7. deduc_____

8. elig_____

9. enforc_____

10. forc_____

11. intellig_____

12. invinc_____

13. knowledg_____

14. leg_____

15. manag_____

16. marriag_____

17. neglig_____

18. produc_____

19. pronounc_____

20. reduc_____

21. servic_____

22. tang_____

23. traduc_____

Answers are on page 33.

1-10. Spelling with *h*'s

Are there any h*'s missing in the words listed? If so, where do they go?*

1. diptheria

2. exilarate

3. exort

4. exorbitant

5. Indira Gandi

6. jodpur

7. naptha

8. silouette

9. threshold

10. withold

Answers are on page 34.

1-11. Adjectives for Proper Nouns

What are the adjective forms of the proper nouns listed? Here's an example: Chaucer, Chaucerian.

1. Afghanistan

2. Barbados

3. Boston

4. Brittany

5. Cambridge

6. Kashmir

7. Lapland

8. Liverpool

9. Malta

10. Quebec

11. Thailand

12. Wales

13. Thomas Aquinas

14. George Gordon, Lord Byron

15. Charlemagne

16. Dante Alighieri

17. René Descartes

18. Moses

19. Napoleon Bonaparte

20. François Rabelais

21. G.B. Shaw

Answers are on page 34.

100 Problem Words

The following are problem words from the standpoint of usage or spelling—sometimes both.
Where not all American authorities agree on a spelling, the most commonly accepted spelling is given.

1. aberration	35. fallout	69. overall
2. a cappella	36. forswear	70. paralleled
3. accommodate	37. fulfill	71. permissible
4. admissible	38. furor	72. perseverance
5. adviser	39. gauge	73. personnel
6. appall	40. genealogy	74. picnicking
7. baccalaureate	41. glamour	75. plethora
8. banknote	42. good-bye	76. potpourri
9. bas-relief	43. goodwill	77. premiere
10. benefited	44. hangar	78. propeller
11. besiege	45. hanged	79. questionnaire
12. bus, buses	46. harass	80. queue
13. caliber	47. harebrained	81. repertory
14. capital (city)	48. heinous	82. retrieve
15. capitol (building)	49. homemade	83. schoolteacher
16. catalog	50. imposter	84. separate
17. cave-in	51. indispensable	85. siege
18. chauffeur	52. infrared	86. sieve
19. consensus	53. innuendo	87. skillful
20. criterion, criteria (plural)	54. innocuous	88. subpoena
21. datum, data	55. inoculate	89. supersede
22. deductible	56. judgment	90. toll bridge
23. defensible	57. kidnapping	91. tonnage
24. desiccate	58. knowledge	92. typing
25. dietitian	59. liaison	93. vacuum
26. dilettante	60. life-size	94. vicissitude
27. drought	61. likable	95. vilify
28. eleemosynary	62. menace	96. weird
29. embarrass	63. mineralogy	97. wield
30. employee	64. missile	98. X-ray
31. endorse	65. misspelled	99. yogurt
32. enforce	66. naive	100. zucchini
33. ensure	67. obbligato	
34. entrepreneur	68. occur	

1-12.   Anatomical Adjectives

Match the adjectives with the nouns in the following lists.

Nouns

1. arm	14. head	
2. back	15. kidney	
3. bladder	16. lip	
4. blood	17. liver	
5. bone	18. mouth	
6. cheek	19. nose	
7. chest	20. skin	
8. ear	21. sole	
9. eyelash	22. tail	
10. foot	23. tongue	
11. forearm	24. tooth	
12. forehead	25. wrist	
13. hair		

Adjectives

a. aural	n. hemal
b. brachial	o. hepatic
c. buccal	p. labial
d. capillary	q. lingual
e. carpal	r. oral
f. caudal	s. osteal
g. cephalic	t. pectoral
h. ciliary	u. pedal
i. cubital	v. plantar
j. dental	w. renal
k. dermal	x. rhinal
l. dorsal	y. vesical
m. frontal	

Answers are on page 35.

1-13. Words Often Misspelled

These words are often misspelled by editors, writers, and college graduates in other professions. Can you find the six we've intentionally misspelled?

1.	achieve	20.	fricassee
2.	algae	21.	fuselage
3.	annihilate	22.	gloat
4.	athlete	23.	gynecologist
5.	broccoli	24.	innoculate
6.	campaign	25.	innocuous
7.	catalyst	26.	knowledge
8.	cemetery	27.	licence
9.	condemn	28.	liquify
10.	croak	29.	millennium
11.	delete	30.	miscellaneous
12.	demagogue	31.	missile
13.	dilapidated	32.	omitted
14.	dissipated	33.	phial
15.	duel	34.	phlegm
16.	ecstasy	35.	prairie
17.	excede	36.	raspberry
18.	facial	37.	sheriff
19.	foreign	38.	sieve

39. sieze

40. spigot

41. subpoena

42. supercede

43. tariff

44. tonsillitis

45. tyranny

46. usage

47. vengeance

48. weird

49. wholly

50. yield

51. zeal

52. zephyr

Answers are on page 35.

Of Gravity, Gold, and Government

Letter by letter, we inventive humans create complexity for ourselves. Take, for example, the letter *g*. On a rainy afternoon, as we were browsing in *Webster's Third New International Dictionary*, we discovered that, in addition to being the seventh letter of the alphabet, *g* is also used to signify a musical note, something designated as the seventh class, something having the shape of the letter *g*, a unit of force applied to a body at rest, a general factor in intelligence meaning *general ability*, and $1,000.

What's more, when used as an abbreviation, *g* (often capped) can stand for game, garage, left (for *gauche* in French), gauge, gauss, gelding, gender, general, genitive, German, gilbert, gilt, glider, gloom, goal/goalie, gold, good, gourde, government, grain, gram, grand, gravity/acceleration of gravity, great, green, Greenwich time, grid, groschen, gross, group, guard, guardian, guide, guilder, guinea, gulden, and gulf. Finally, *g* may be used, often capped, as a symbol for conductance.

1-14   Plurals of Nouns Ending in *f*

What are the plurals of the following nouns?

1.	beef	6.	scarf
2.	leaf	7.	staff
3.	belief	8.	turf
4.	hoof	9.	wharf
5.	dwarf	10.	roof

Answers are on page 36.

Abbreviations/Acronyms/Initialisms

Abbreviation is the general term for a shortened form of a name or word, such as *FL* or *Fla.* for *Florida*. Abbreviations were devised by early scribes and typesetters to save time and space. Most abbreviations should be defined at first use in text; exceptions are those standing for words rarely seen spelled out (*Mr., Mrs., Dr., Ph.D., A.M., P.M., RSVP,* and the like).

An *acronym* is composed of the opening letters of a group of words. Unlike an abbreviation, an acronym is *not* simply a collection of capital letters that stand for something: For example, *RCA* stands for Radio Corporation of America, but it isn't an acronym. An acronym must be pronounceable as a word. Thus,

NATO and *SALT* are acronyms, while *EPA, CBS,* and *OMB* (and *RCA*) are abbreviations. Some people use the term *initialism* to mean an abbreviation composed of the initial letters (or syllables) of the words in a name or term but pronounced letter by letter.

Over time, an acronym may completely supplant the words it used to represent, as in the case of *radar* (radio detecting and ranging) and *modem* (modulator demodulator). The wish for a snappy acronym has led some groups to devise one first and then make the spelled-out version fit the letters: *MADD* (Mothers Against Drunk Driving) is a good example.

Acronyms and initialisms are widely used to represent

- organizations (*CARE, UNICEF, NATO, UL*-approved),
- medical and scientific terms (*MMPI, AIDS, mph*),
- computer systems and processes (*DOS, WYSIWYG, ASCII*), and
- conversational shorthand (*AWOL, COB, ASAP*).

The most comprehensive reference work for what abbreviations mean, with 480,000 definitions, is the *Acronyms, Initialisms, and Abbreviations Dictionary,* published by Gale Research (Detroit) and updated periodically.

1-15. Forming Plurals

Write the plural form for each of the following words.

Compound Words

1. assistant attorney general

2. bill of fare

3. chaise longue

4. commander in chief

5. court-martial

6. crepe suzette

7. foothold

8. go-between

9. looker-on

10. notary public

11. standby

12. talisman

13. time-out

Abbreviations

14. PTA

15. V.P.

16. c.o.d.

Miscellaneous

17. yes and no

18. do and don't

19. 10

20. cupful

21. soliloquy

Answers are on page 36.

1-16. Common Abbreviations and Their Alternative Forms

Some commonly accepted abbreviations turn up just infrequently enough to give us pause when we encounter them; others are a problem when we have to read unfamiliar material. Also, some abbreviations (especially the medical ones) have alternative forms (often with periods or without).

What do these abbreviations stand for?

1.	a.	17.	hhd.
2.	ATV	18.	ISBN
3.	bbl.	19.	l/min
4.	B.C.E.	20.	L/s
5.	C	21.	MP, mp
6.	C.	22.	MS, ms.; MSS, mss.
7.	Cal	23.	NM
8.	cal, c	24.	NSQ
9.	cc	25.	PERT
10.	cf.	26.	PITI
11.	CLIN	27.	PRN, p.r.n.
12.	f., ff.	28.	RFD
13.	FICA	29.	sc
14.	f.o.b.	30.	SI
15.	f/x	31.	TID, T.I.D., tid, t.i.d.
16.	GMT		

Answers are on page 38.

1-17. Latin Abbreviations and Terms

Give an acceptable English substitute for each of the following Latin abbreviations and terms. (Note that all except the last one are now considered anglicized—that is, they are no longer italicized.)

1. e.g.

2. et al.

3. et seq.

4. ibid.

5. id.

6. i.e.

7. loc. cit.

8. N.B.

9. op. cit.

10. q.v.

11. sc.

12. s.v.

13. viz.

14. ad hominem

15. a posteriori

16. a priori

17. ceteris paribus

18. de novo

19. in extenso

20. in extremis

21. infra

22. modus operandi

23. pari passu

24. passim

25. per contra

26. supra

27. *sic*

Answers are on page 39.

1-18.   Common Statistical Abbreviations

What do they stand for?

1.	ANOVA	12.	min
2.	cdf	13.	MLE
3.	cf	14.	MSE
4.	df	15.	OLS
5.	exp	16.	pdf
6.	iid	17.	plim
7.	iff	18.	rhs
8.	LIML	19.	RMSE
9.	ln	20.	2SLS
10.	log	21.	UMP
11.	max	22.	var

Answers are on page 40.

1-19. Trade Names

Do you know which words are trade names and which can be used generically?
Looking in a dictionary may not give you a clear-cut answer because different sources
give different renderings. Try your hand at capitalizing the words in the following list
that represent specific trade names.

1.	aspirin	18.	frigidaire
2.	baggies	19.	jeep
3.	band-aid	20.	kitty litter
4.	camcorder	21.	kleenex
5.	crock-pot	22.	krazy glue
6.	dacron	23.	laser printer
7.	diet coke	24.	laserjet
8.	disposal	25.	laundromat
9.	disposall	26.	magic marker
10.	dixie cup	27.	mailgram
11.	dramamine	28.	mcintosh apples
12.	dumpster	29.	nylon
13.	e-mail	30.	penicillin
14.	elmer's glue	31.	photocopy
15.	express mail	32.	photostat
16.	fax	33.	ping-pong
17.	formica	34.	popsicle

Continued on next page

35. quonset hut

36. real estate agent

37. refrigerator

38. rollerblades

39. scotch tape

40. tabasco sauce

41. teleprinter

42. teletype

43. telex

44. tylenol

45. valium

46. voice mail

47. walkman stereo

Answers are on page 40.

International Trademark Association (INTA) Guidelines

Every writer should remember to use trademarks as proper adjectives, not as generic lowercased nouns (*Kleenex tissues,* not *kleenex*). Follow spelling and capitalization exactly. (It's not necessary to use ™ or ®, unless you're the trademark holder.) Don't use trademarks as verbs in writing. For example, *Photostat, Xerox, Mace, Simonize,* and *Spackle* frequently—and wrongly—appear in print as verbs.

Because people actively resist constraints against expedient and inventive usage, protecting trademarks is an uphill battle, and even with the best intentions it can be hard to know what constitutes acceptable use of a trademark.

According to the INTA checklist, *Boogie* is a trademark for surfboards. But *The American Heritage Dictionary of the English Language,* 3rd edition (*AHD*), which lists many trademarks, says *boogie* is both a noun and a verb that means "dancing to rock music."

The INTA says *Heimlich Maneuver* should be followed by the phrase *anti-choking educational services. AHD,* however, doesn't capitalize *maneuver* and doesn't list it as a trademark, but rather defines it as an emergency technique devised by Dr. Henry Heimlich—and that's the way most of us use it.

Although *Colorization* is a specific trademark for film conversion services, *colorize* is a generic verb used within the film industry itself and defined in *AHD* as "the imparting of color to black-and-white film by a computer-assisted process."

1-20. Words for Measurements

What do the following units measure?

1. lumen
2. maxwell
3. gauss
4. ohm
5. roentgen
6. volt
7. hertz
8. farad
9. erg
10. angstrom
11. kelvin
12. stoke

Answers are on page 42.

Treat Proper Names Properly

E.B. White once wrote to his biographer, Professor Scott Elledge, "The only real trouble you got into in your piece was when you tried to spell Katharine. My wife does not take any variations lying down."

People may not like the names their parents gave them, but by golly they want them spelled right.

Take care when dealing with names. Look up or check on people's names, particularly uncommon or unfamiliar ones. If you find a name spelled more than one way, don't assume that the most frequent spelling is the correct one.

Be aware that variations on standard spellings and newly coined names abound and seem to be increasing.

Also, be sensitive to people's preferences. Remember that some people choose to use nicknames or names other than those on their birth certificates.

1-21. Verifying Proper Names

Here are some common trademarks and company names for you to check for spelling, capitalization, and punctuation.

1. Anheuser-Busch
2. Astroturf
3. BreathAlyzer
4. Chanel No. 5
5. CinemaScope
6. Compuserve
7. Cool Whip
8. Cut-Rite
9. Day-Glo
10. d-BASE IV
11. Dow-Jones Average
12. Dow Jones Co.
13. Dr Pepper
14. duPont Co.
15. Dun and Bradstreet
16. Elastoplast
17. Etch a Sketch
18. EtherNet
19. FEDEX

20. Fisher Price
21. Freon
22. Gulf + Western
23. Häagen-Dazs
24. Harper Collins
25. Harrods
26. Jack Daniel's
27. Jell-O
28. Jockey shorts
29. Junglegym
30. Kahlua
31. Land-Rover
32. Levi's
33. LinoType
34. Liquid Plumber
35. MacIntosh
36. MicroSoft Word
37. Mini Cam
38. Miracle-Gro

39. Mr. Coffee

40. Muzak

41. Nescafé

42. NFL Players Association

43. Page Maker

44. Photo Stat

45. Play-Doh

46. Plexiglas

47. Poloroid

48. Pop-Tart

49. Post-It

50. Ray-Ban

51. REALtor

52. Reddi Wip

53. Rolls-Royce

54. Rolodex

55. S.A.T.

56. S & P 500

57. Screen Actors Guild

58. Seeing-Eye (dog)

59. SheetRock

60. SuperGlue

61. TelePrompTer

62. 3-M Co.

63. TouchTone

64. Twentieth Century-Fox

65. the "21" Club

66. VuGraph

67. Word Perfect

68. XActo

69. Xerox

Answers are on page 42.

1-1. Judge Your Spelling Expertise

1. **Supersede.**

2. **Exceed, proceed, succeed.** All other "seed" words end in *-cede*: **intercede, secede, concede,** and so on.

3. To keep the hard *c* sound, words ending in *c* usually add a *k* before a suffix beginning with a vowel: **mimicked.**

4. According to *Merriam-Webster's Collegiate Dictionary*, 10th edition (*Webster's 10th*), both **bused** and **bussed** are acceptable.

5. *Webster's 10th* lists **judgment** first but accepts both spellings; **judgment** is preferable in the United States, **judgement** in Britain.

6. Musical terms ending in *o* form their plurals by adding *s*: **altos, banjos, cellos.** As for the other words, some add *s* (**hairdos, radios, tattoos**), some add *es* (**tomatoes, heroes**), and some give you a choice (**ghettos** or **ghettoes, cargos** or **cargoes, zeros** or **zeroes, noes** or **nos**). Only your dictionary knows for sure.

7. Most nouns ending in a *y* preceded by a vowel form their plurals by adding *s*, although there are some exceptions: **soliloquies,** for example.

8. Generally, pluralize the chief element of hyphenated words and compound words that aren't joined by hyphens: **daughters-in-law, runners-up, deputy chiefs of staff, lieutenant generals** (but **courts-martial** or **court-martials, notaries public** or **notary publics, attorneys general** or **attorney generals**). Generally, pluralize the final element of solid compounds: **forefeet, mousetraps** (**passersby** is an exception). Plurals of hyphenated compounds that don't contain nouns are formed by pluralizing the final element: **hand-me-downs.**

9. Most surnames are pluralized by adding *s*. The spelling shouldn't be changed. Add *es* to surnames that end in *s, ch, sh, x,* or *i*: **Crosbys** (not **Crosbies**), **Wolfs** (not **Wolves**), **Continettis, Friedmans** (not **Friedmen**), **Foxes, Joneses, Matises, Bartinos.**

10. First names are made plural by adding *s* or *es*. The spelling shouldn't be changed: **Sandis, Marys, Jameses, Ottos.**

11. Proper nouns are made plural by adding *s* or *es*, and the spelling usually doesn't change: **Carolinas, Januarys. Alleghenies** and **Rockies** are exceptions.

1-2. *ei* or *ie*?

1. seize	18. deign
2. siege	19. yield
3. sieve	20. foreign
4. bier	21. grieve
5. tier	22. deceive
6. mien	23. achieve
7. vein	24. believe
8. view	25. neither
9. height	26. ancient
10. sleigh	27. heinous
11. weight	28. forfeit
12. weir	29. leisure
13. weird	30. inveigle
14. piece	31. ceiling
15. niece	32. receipt
16. friend	33. sheik
17. fiend	34. shriek

1-3. The Prefix *for-* vs. *fore-*

1. forbid	8. forgive
2. forebode	9. forgo (do without)
3. forecast	forego (go before)
4. foreclose	10. forlorn
5. forfeit	11. forsworn★
6. forgather★	12. foretell
7. forget	13. forward
	14. foreword

★Some dictionaries also accept *fore-* as a prefix to these words.

1-4. The Suffixes *-acy, -asy, -esy,* and *-isy*

1. advocacy	7. efficacy
2. apostasy	8. hypocrisy
3. courtesy	9. idiosyncrasy
4. delicacy	10. pleurisy
5. diplomacy	11. profligacy
6. ecstasy	12. supremacy

1-5. The Suffix *-ly* vs. *-ally*

Only one of the words requires *–ly* instead of *–ally*: *publicly*. For *frantic*, dictionaries accept both *frantically* and *franticly* as correct.

1. angelically	16. fanatically
2. apologetically	17. frantically or franticly
3. artistically	18. graphically
4. basically	19. heroically
5. catastrophically	20. historically
6. climatically	21. laconically
7. clinically	22. lethargically
8. cynically	23. logically
9. diabolically	24. organically
10. dogmatically	25. prolifically
11. dramatically	26. publicly
12. eccentrically	27. rhythmically
13. empirically	28. specifically
14. energetically	29. systematically
15. ethically	30. tragically

1-6. The Suffix *-eous* vs. *-ious*

1. b. audacious
2. a. bounteous
3. b. crustaceous
4. b. disputatious
5. b. facetious
6. b. herbaceous
7. b. loquacious
8. a. ostentatious
9. a. salacious
10. b. tenacious
11. b. tendentious

1-7. The Suffix *-or* vs. *-er*

Norman Lewis, author of *Correct Spelling Made Easy*, says that when we stop and think about the endings of words such as *butcher*, *bettor*, and *registrar*, "we're lost, because if we don't reflexively and self-confidently tack the proper suffix to a root, *-er* and *-or* suddenly seem equally good." That's what personal style sheets are for: doubtful moments.

1. accelerator
2. administrator
3. burglar
4. propeller or propellor
5. elevator
6. engraver
7. escalator
8. fabricator
9. gossiper
10. indicator
11. investigator
12. orator
13. transgressor
14. prisoner
15. supervisor
16. Procter & Gamble

1-8. The Suffixes *-ary*, *-ery*, and *-ory*

1. thievery
2. auxiliary
3. brewery
4. distillery
5. flattery
6. mockery
7. hereditary
8. necessary
9. summary*
10. cemetery
11. dictionary
12. monastery
13. chicanery
14. complimentary
15. confectionery
16. documentary
17. dysentery
18. elementary
19. exemplary
20. fiduciary
21. imaginary
22. parliamentary
23. promissory
24. rudimentary
25. salary
26. statutory

*Also *summery*, as in "summer-like."

1-9. The Suffixes *-able*, *-eable*, and *-ible*

1. challengeable
2. changeable
3. chargeablc
4. coercible
5. corrigible
6. damageable
7. deducible
8. eligible
9. enforceable
10. forcible
11. intelligible
12. invincible
13. knowledgeable
14. legible
15. manageable
16. marriageable
17. negligible
18. producible
19. pronounceable
20. reducible
21. serviceable
22. tangible
23. traducible

1-10.   Spelling with *h*'s

1. diphtheria
2. exhilarate
3. exhort
4. correct as is
5. Indira Gandhi
6. jodhpur
7. naphtha
8. silhouette
9. correct as is
10. withhold

1-11.   Adjectives for Proper Nouns

1. Afghan
2. Barbadian, Bajan
3. Bostonian
4. Breton
5. Cantabrigian
6. Kashmiri
7. Lapp
8. Liverpudlian
9. Maltese
10. Quebecer, Quebecker, Québecois, Québecoise
11. Thai
12. Welsh
13. Thomist
14. Byronic
15. Caroline, Carolingian
16. Dantesque
17. Cartesian
18. Mosaic
19. Napoleonic
20. Rabelaisian
21. Shavian

1-12. Anatomical Adjectives

1.	b.	brachial	14.	g.	cephalic
2.	l.	dorsal	15.	w.	renal
3.	y.	vesical	16.	p.	labial
4.	n.	hemal	17.	o.	hepatic
5.	s.	osteal	18.	r.	oral
6.	c.	buccal	19.	x.	rhinal
7.	t.	pectoral	20.	k.	dermal
8.	a.	aural	21.	v.	plantar
9.	h.	ciliary	22.	f.	caudal
10.	u.	pedal	23.	q.	lingual
11.	i.	cubital	24.	j.	dental
12.	m.	frontal	25.	e.	carpal
13.	d.	capillary			

1-13. Words Often Misspelled

Here are the correct spellings for the six misspelled words:

17.	exceed	28.	liquefy
24.	inoculate	39.	seize
27.	license	42.	supersede

1-14. Plurals of Nouns Ending in *f*

We derived these answers from *Merriam-Webster's Collegiate Dictionary*, 10th edition.

1. beef, beefs, beeves
2. leaves
3. beliefs
4. hooves, hoofs
5. dwarfs, dwarves

6. scarves, scarfs
7. staffs, staves
8. turfs, turves
9. wharves, wharfs
10. roofs

1-15. Forming Plurals

The answers are based on *The New York Public Library Writer's Guide to Style and Usage (NYPL)* and *The Gregg Reference Manual*, 8th edition *(Gregg)*. See the footnote for rules.

Type	Singular	Plural	Rule/Reference
Compound Words The numbers and their sources listed in the Rule/Reference column at far right refer to the footnote to the table. If only one source is listed for a particular plural, that source is indicated; if the sources disagree, both plurals are given.	1. assistant attorney general	assistant attorneys general assistant attorneys general or assistant attorney generals	1—*NYPL* 4—*Gregg*
	2. bill of fare	bills of fare	1—*NYPL*
	3. chaise longue	chaise longues	Exception to 2—*Gregg* (Note: Correct spelling is *longues*, not *lounges*)
	4. commander in chief	commanders in chief	1—*NYPL*
	5. court-martial	courts-martial courts-martial or court-martials	1—*NYPL* 4—*Gregg*
	6. crepe suzette	crepes suzette	1—*NYPL*
	7. foothold	footholds	1—*Gregg*
	8. go-between	go-betweens	Same for both
	9. looker-on	lookers-on	Same for both
	10. notary public	notaries public notaries public or notary publics	1—*NYPL* 4—*Gregg*
	11. standby	standbys	1—*Gregg*
	12. talisman	talismans	Exception to 1—*Gregg*
	13. time-out	time-outs	Exception to 2, 3—*NYPL* Exception to 2, 3—*Gregg*

Type	Singular	Plural	Rule/Reference
Abbreviations	14. PTA	PTAs	According to *Gregg*, abbreviations with capital letters are pluralized by adding *s* alone. Lower-cased abbreviations are pluralized by adding *'s*. Some styles use an apostrophe after all abbreviations to indicate the plural.
	15. V.P.	V.P.s	
	16. c.o.d.	c.o.d.'s	
Miscellaneous	17. yes and no	yeses and noes	According to *Gregg*, words taken from other parts of speech and used as nouns are usually pluralized by adding *s* or *es*.
	18. do and don't	dos and don'ts	
	19. 10	10s	When pluralizing figures, simply add *s*. (There are exceptions; the *U.S. Government Printing Office Style Manual* adds *'s*: *10's*.)
	20. cupful	cupfuls	Nouns ending in *-ful* are pluralized by adding *s*. (*Five cupfuls of sugar* is a quantity of sugar that would fill a cup five times, while *five cups full of sugar* means five separate cups each filled with sugar. *Cupsful* is not a word.)
	21. soliloquy	soliloquies	Nouns that end in a *y* preceded by a vowel form the plural by adding *s*. According to *NYPL*, "an exception is the *qu-* combination, which is treated like a consonant in forming the plural."

NYPL:

1. "…the most significant word—generally the noun—takes the plural form. This word may be at the beginning, middle, or end of the term."
2. "When no single word is of great significance or when neither word is a noun, the plural is formed on the last word."
3. "When a noun is joined with an adverb or preposition with a hyphen, the plural is formed on the noun."

Gregg:

1. "When a compound noun is a solid word, pluralize the final element in the compound as if it stood alone."
2. "The plurals of hyphenated or spaced compounds are formed by pluralizing the chief element of the compound."
3. "When a hyphenated compound does not contain a noun as one of its elements, simply pluralize the final element."
4. "Some of these…compounds have two recognized plural forms."

ANSWERS

1-16. Common Abbreviations and Their Alternative Forms

1. acre
2. all-terrain vehicle
3. barrel
4. before the Christian (or common) era
5. centigrade, Celsius; coulomb
6. curie
7. large calorie (kilocalorie)
8. calorie
9. cubic centimeter
10. compare
11. contract line item number
12. and following, pages following
13. Federal Insurance Contributions Act (Social Security)
14. free (or freight) on board
15. special effects (movies)
16. Greenwich mean time
17. hogshead
18. International Standard Book Number
19. lines per minute
20. liters per second
21. melting point
22. manuscript; manuscripts
23. nautical mile
24. not sufficient quantity
25. program evaluation and review technique
26. principal, interest, taxes, and insurance
27. pro re nata (L., as the occasion arises; when necessary)
28. rural free delivery
29. small capital letters; subcutaneous
30. International System of Units (Fr., Système International d'Unités)
31. ter in die (L., three times daily)

1-17. Latin Abbreviations and Terms

1.   (exempli gratia) for example

2.   (et alia) and others; (et alibi) and elsewhere

3.   (et sequens) and the following

4.   (ibidem) in the same place

5.   (idem) the same

6.   (id est) that is

7.   (loco citato) in the place cited

8.   (nota bene) note well

9.   (opere citato) in the work cited

10. (quod vide) which see

11. (scilicet) namely

12. (sub verbo) under a word; (sub voce) heading

13. (videlicet) namely

14. appealing to feelings or prejudices rather than to the intellect; in logic, a supposed argument against something but in fact an attack on the person rather than the merits of the person's position

15. inductive

16. deductive; presumptive

17. other things being equal

18. over again; anew

19. at full length

20. in extreme circumstances; at the point of death

21. below

22. method or procedure

23. at an equal rate or pace

24. here and there, used particularly in footnote references when no specific page reference is given

25. on the contrary

26. above

27. thus

1-18.   Common Statistical Abbreviations

1. analysis of variance
2. cumulative distribution function
3. continuous function
4. degrees of freedom
5. exponential
6. identically and independently distributed
7. if and only if
8. limited-information maximum likelihood
9. natural logarithm
10. logarithm
11. maximum
12. minimum
13. maximum likelihood estimator
14. mean squared error
15. ordinary least squares
16. probability density function
17. probability at the limit
18. right-hand side
19. root mean square error
20. two-stage least squares
21. uniform most powerful
22. variance

1-19.   Trade Names

Several sources were consulted to find these answers: *The Gregg Reference Manual*, 8th edition (*Gregg*); the *United States Government Printing Office Style Manual,* which gives a list of trade names in its Guide to Capitalization (pages 58–59); and *The Chicago Manual of Style*, 14th edition, which states the following on page 282: "Dictionaries indicate registered trademark names. A reasonable effort should be made to capitalize such names." *The American Heritage Dictionary of the English Language,* 3rd edition (*AHD*) offered these distinctions:

- trademark (TM)—"a name, symbol, or other device identifying a product, officially registered and legally restricted to the use of the owner or manufacturer."

- trade name—"a name used to identify a commercial product or service, which may or may not be registered as a trademark."

- service mark (SM)—"a mark used in the sale or advertising of services to identify the services and distinguish them from services of others."

In most cases *AHD* agreed with *Gregg*, but not all terms were listed, and some were listed differently: *AHD* lists *Jeep* but also *jeep; KITTY LITTER; Tabasco sauce* but also *tabasco pepper; Walkman* without *stereo*.

1.	aspirin	25.	Laundromat
2.	Baggies	26.	Magic Marker
3.	Band-Aid	27.	Mailgram
4.	camcorder	28.	McIntosh apples
5.	Crock-Pot	29.	nylon
6.	Dacron	30.	penicillin
7.	diet Coke	31.	photocopy
8.	disposal	32.	Photostat
9.	Disposall	33.	Ping-Pong
10.	Dixie cup	34.	Popsicle
11.	Dramamine	35.	Quonset hut
12.	Dumpster	36.	real estate agent
13.	E-mail	37.	refrigerator
14.	Elmer's glue	38.	Rollerblades
15.	Express Mail	39.	Scotch tape
16.	fax	40.	Tabasco sauce
17.	Formica	41.	teleprinter
18.	Frigidaire	42.	Teletype
19.	Jeep	43.	telex
20.	Kitty Litter	44.	Tylenol
21.	Kleenex	45.	Valium
22.	Krazy Glue	46.	voice mail
23.	laser printer	47.	Walkman stereo
24.	LaserJet		

1-20. Words for Measurements

1. electromagnetic radiation flux

2. magnetic flux

3. magnetic induction (a maxwell/cm^2)

4. electrical resistance

5. the quantity of X-rays or gamma rays

6. electromotive force

7. cycles of electrical frequency per second

8. electrical capacitance

9. work or energy

10. length (10^{-10}m; usually used to measure light wavelengths)

11. temperature

12. viscosity

1-21. Verifying Proper Names

These answers were drawn from *The New York Public Library Writer's Guide to Style and Usage*; *Words Into Type*; *Proper Noun Speller* (Los Angeles: Quickref Publishing, 1990); and the *United States Government Printing Office Style Manual*.

1. Anheuser-Busch

2. Astroturf

3. Breathalyzer

4. Chanel No. 5

5. CinemaScope

6. CompuServe

7. Cool Whip

8. Cut-Rite

9. Day-Glo

10. d-BASE IV

11. Dow Jones Average

12. Dow Jones & Co.

13. Dr Pepper

14. DuPont (but E.I. du Pont de Nemours and Company)

15. Dun & Bradstreet

16. Elastoplast

17. Etch a Sketch

18. Ethernet

19. FedEx

20. Fisher-Price

21. Freon

22.	Gulf + Western	46.	Plexiglas
23.	Häagen-Dazs	47.	Polaroid
24.	HarperCollins	48.	Pop-Tart
25.	Harrods	49.	Post-it
26.	Jack Daniel's	50.	Ray-Ban
27.	Jell-O	51.	Realtor
28.	Jockey shorts	52.	Reddi Wip
29.	jungle gym★	53.	Rolls-Royce
30.	Kahlua	54.	Rolodex
31.	Land-Rover	55.	SAT
32.	Levi's	56.	S & P 500
33.	Linotype	57.	Screen Actors Guild
34.	Liquid Plumr	58.	Seeing Eye (dog)
35.	Macintosh computer	59.	Sheetrock
36.	Microsoft Word	60.	Super glue
37.	Minicam	61.	TelePrompTer
38.	Miracle-Gro	62.	3M Co.
39.	Mr. Coffee	63.	Touch-Tone
40.	Muzak	64.	Twentieth Century-Fox
41.	Nescafé	65.	the "21" Club
42.	NFL Players Association	66.	Vu-Graph
43.	PageMaker	67.	WordPerfect
44.	Photostat	68.	X-Acto
45.	Play-Doh	69.	Xerox
			(always capped, *never* a verb)

★This trademark has been lost! Just testing your reflexes.

PUNCTUATION

Punctuation is more subjective than spelling: it's easy to check whether a word is spelled according to the dictionary or not. Also, styles of punctuation may vary somewhat with the taste of the individual writer and with the type of style guide a publication uses. Clear, consistent punctuation—not too much and not too little—is just as basic to good writing as accurate spelling is.

This chapter deals with the appropriate use of punctuation, from essential and nonessential commas to semicolons, quotation marks, dashes, parentheses, and of course those ever-troublesome apostrophes. The text also points out acceptable choices, explaining what's common to every punctuation style and what's specific to the journalistic, scientific, humanistic, and other styles.

2-1. Punctuation Grab Bag

If the punctuation in the following sentences is correct, mark the sentence with a C. If the punctuation is incorrect, fix it.

1. Why Yvonne Ryder left this agency so quickly has never been explained?

2. How do you explain this comment on the manuscript: "This editor does not do bibliographies"?

3. All employees, who want to enroll for automatic deposit, must complete the appropriate forms by the end of this month.

4. Our employees, who are already entitled to many medical benefits, will now be entitled to parking and cafeteria privileges.

5. The supervisor of the graphics department is ill, nevertheless, the project was completed as scheduled.

6. We are convinced, however, that we can meet the client's specifications for this software manual.

7. The senior managers have requested that you Ms. Conners be in charge of the new resources library.

Answers are on page 67.

What's a Virgule For?

The virgule, a simple punctuation mark (/), has more than a half-dozen names, but nowhere near that many proper uses. It's sometimes called the *diagonal, solidus, slash, slant, shill,* or *shilling,* but its true function is best remembered by the name *separatrix,* because the mark is used primarily to show separation or division.

Thus, the virgule may separate run-in lines of poetry, represent *per* in expressions like *50 km/hr,* and separate day, month, and year in abbreviated forms like *6/25/91.* It is sometimes used to indicate a period of time extending over two calendar years (*winter 1997/98*) or days (*June 5/6*) or alternative spellings (*Raleigh/Ralegh*). But the mark shouldn't be used in expressions like *The editor wanted to reject and/or rewrite the manuscript,* where use of the virgule is symptomatic of hazy thinking. If you're not sure whether you mean *and* or *or,* you need to rethink the whole sentence.

2-2. Help Stop Comma Litter

Do you add commas uncertainly, thinking, "It seems that a comma should go there, but I'm not sure why"? It pays to have a reason for every comma you use. As you insert commas in the following sentences, keep in mind that some commas are necessary while others are simply litter.

1. The seminars will be conducted every Saturday from August 1 1998 until November 30 1998 at the town hall; certificates will be mailed in January 1999.

2. Because we must meet our Friday deadline we have hired temporary employees to get us through the "crunch."

3. My father Robert Smith III and my grandfather Robert Smith Jr. have both decided to toss their hats into the political arena.

4. The wisecrack "Men seldom make passes at girls who wear glasses" is attributed to Dorothy Parker.

5. Traffic in the area is usually congested but since the new construction work has begun on the bridge into the city rush hour has become a nightmare.

6. Although I was offered a good position at a small newly created privately owned company I chose to accept an offer from a large well-known well-established nonprofit organization.

7. The candidates who received last-minute funds from local PACs for a media blitz plan to saturate the airwaves before election day.

8. The bicycle which was left in the driveway was stolen last night.

9. The bicycle that was left in the driveway was stolen last night.

10. Recognizing your own weaknesses as well as your strengths will help you advance in your career.

Answers are on page 68.

2-3. Punctuation with Conjunctions

"My sixth-grade teacher told me to always put a comma before and *in a compound sentence." "I was taught never to use a comma in a compound sentence." "I know a comma should always be placed after* but." *"I think* but *should be preceded and followed by a comma." "The word* however *is always preceded by a semicolon, but the word* but *never follows a semicolon."*

This test is designed to debunk some myths and set the record straight. Although the rules for semicolons are fairly straightforward, comma usage is complex and in flux. Many people use commas where a speaker would normally pause, and in some cases this usage is correct. The rules for commas are sometimes based on grammar and sometimes on style. Use of commas can be optional, especially for compound sentences.

Some sentences are compound-complex, a sentence form used sparingly in the real world for good reason: It's hard to write well and can be hard to understand. Rewrite such sentences whenever you can.

With all this in mind, add or delete punctuation as necessary for the following coordinate, correlative, and subordinate conjunctions and conjunctive adverbs. (If your mythical memory is short, cheat and check the list of conjunctive adverbs in item 3 of the answers on page 70.)

Note: *Many of the example sentences were borrowed from* Writing Mysteries: A Handbook *by the Mystery Writers of America (Cincinnati: Writer's Digest Books, 1992).*

1. As a young writer, Bella ghosted for several mystery writers, and she now feels that this "ghosting" was more valuable than anything she learned in the classroom.

2. Bella ghosted for several mystery writers, and has always felt that this "ghosting" was more valuable than anything she learned in the classroom.

3. A private investigation novel, by its very nature, requires some violence, however, the trick is to make the violence rational, and thus, advance the plot.

4. Medical research oddities, political trivia or reports of unusual psychic, or extraterrestrial events can trigger the beginning of an idea.

5. Sometimes an amateur sleuth becomes involved in a case at the request of a friend. Or, maybe the sleuth is just naturally curious.

6. Orient your reader to the locale and use background to your advantage.

7. Avoid creating a villain who is more interesting than the protagonist because the plot will be lopsided.

8. When we speak of something that did not exist before we are referring to an *invention* but when we speak of something that did exist before but was not known we are referring to a *discovery*.

9. We requested information on patent attorneys qualifications for applying for a patent and the length of time for which a patent is valid but information on royalties patents in other countries and the history of the United States Patent Office was sent instead.

10. After you are granted a patent you may sell the rights to a manufacturer or you may license your rights—that is you may allow a company to make or sell your invention in return for royalties.

11. It is legal not only to patent an invention but also to patent an improvement on an already existing device or machine.

12. A modern jet with its hundreds of comfortable seats and movies and lavatories and kitchens hardly compares with the Wright brothers' biplane, in which a single pilot lay on his stomach with the wind gusting all around him.

Answers are on page 70.

2-4. Punctuating Restrictive/Nonrestrictive Elements

Think of the pair of commas around nonrestrictive elements as handles that can be used to lift the phrase or clause out of the sentence. If the sentence doesn't make sense when the phrase is removed, then the information is necessary, or restrictive *(essential, definitive). Commas should* not *be used to set off restrictive information.*

If the meaning of the sentence is clear and complete after the information is lifted out, then the information is unnecessary; it is nonrestrictive *(nonessential, extraneous). Set off nonrestrictive information with commas.*

Often, the key to deciding whether to use commas is deciding whether an element is a restrictive appositive—*a noun that means the same as another noun or creates an identity—or merely adds information.*

Remember that an element can be a word, a phrase, or a clause that describes, explains, or defines another element. A restrictive clause is usually introduced by *that and isn't set off by commas, whereas a nonrestrictive clause is introduced by* which *and does have commas.*

Decide whether information is restrictive or nonrestrictive in these sentences, and add commas where appropriate.

Note: *Some of these sentences were adapted from* The New Book of Knowledge, *Vol. 14 (Danbury, CT: Grolier Inc., 1989).*

1. Until recently, the modern Olympic Games that were begun in Athens, Greece, in 1896 were held during the last year of each Olympiad—a period of four years ending in a leap year.

2. During the Golden Age of Greece, the great poet, Pindar, wrote odes in honor of the winners, who were presented with a laurel or wild olive wreath.

3. *Stadium* is derived from the Greek word, *stadion*, which is a unit of measure equal to about 190 meters, the length of the first footraces.

4. Only free male citizens were permitted to participate in the games; women were forbidden on penalty of death to even see them.

5. Milo, a wrestler in the sixth century B.C., who won the wrestling crown six times, has often been considered the greatest athlete of ancient times.

6. The competition, added in 1924, included cold-weather sports and became known as the Winter Games.

7. At the 1936 Olympic Games, the dictator, Adolf Hitler, refused to acknowledge the triumphs of Jesse Owens, a black American sprinter and long jumper.

8. The International Olympic Committee organized in 1894 by Baron de Coubertin governs the Games and works with the national committees that must avoid any commercial, religious, or political interference.

9. The spectator, who was shooting a video of Nancy Kerrigan, an Olympic hopeful, caught on tape a man, holding a club while watching Kerrigan skate.

Answers are on page 73.

Rules for Commas with Modifiers

A standard approach for deciding whether to use a comma between compound adjectives is this: If the phrase would make sense with *and*, insert a comma. Using that test on the phrase *high-interest short-term bank bonds*, the term *high-interest and short-term* clearly makes sense, but *short-term and bank* doesn't, thus *high-interest, short-term bank bonds*.

There's also a second standard test: Change the order of the adjectives. If the switched version would have the same meaning and "sounds" like something someone would say, use a comma. Testing, *short-term high-interest bank bonds* sounded fine; *short-term bank high-interest bonds* seemed libelous; and *bank short-term high-interest bonds* was patently foolish. Thus,

again, *high-interest, short-term bank bonds*.

Both tests rely on judgment to interpret the results, and that's not such a bad thing. Still, neither test explained why to add the comma or why not to use two. Here are some guidelines:

• First and foremost, distinguish between coordinate, cumulative, and attributive modifiers:
  — **Coordinate modifiers** are of roughly equal weight; they can be joined by *and* or by a comma and can usually be switched around without damage to meaning.
  — **Cumulative modifiers** build up to the noun; rearranging the words or adding *and* or a comma yields nonsense.

  — **Attributive modifiers** (nouns that modify other nouns) are so closely linked to the modified noun that they're treated as being part of a compound; they're not preceded by a comma.
• A number (cardinal or ordinal) goes at the beginning of the adjectival phrase and is virtually never followed by a comma.
• Regardless of the number or type of adjectives, the noun is never preceded by a comma. This is true for simple nouns and for compound nouns, such as *vice president*.
• If there are only two simple adjectives, the phrase is often fine without a comma.

2-5.   Commas with Compound Adjectives

Years ago, there was a popular song about a "one-eyed, one-horned, flying purple people-eater." (If you're old enough to remember it, you're probably humming it already.) The phrase high-interest short-term bank bonds *brings that song to mind. To comma or not? Even with simple adjectives, deciding when to use a comma is sometimes a puzzle. With compound adjectives, the puzzle often seems more challenging.*

Ready to try your hand? Add commas as appropriate.

1.   Somehow, Sandy was not persuaded by the widely held childhood belief in a beautiful open-handed tooth fairy; that first little incisor never did get put under the pillow.

2.   Lee, a hard-working interior designer with a talented long-suffering staff, had to make the best of a bad situation while dealing with three work-related disasters in one exhausting week.

3.   The project managers relied on a well-known cost-free data source as they outlined the report for their most important new client.

4.   The question is this: Should less-productive agricultural land in played-out marginal areas be taxed at the same high rate as fields that yield bumper crops?

5.   Go ahead and eat your nice juicy steak, darling; I'll be perfectly happy with a cool crisp salad.

Answers are on page 75.

2-6.   Essential Series Commas

Journalistic style guides, such as the Associated Press Stylebook and Libel Manual (AP)*, say that the serial or series comma—the comma before the final conjunction in a list of items such as* red, white, and blue*—is unnecessary except when confusion would result without it. Other guides, such as* The Chicago Manual of Style, *14th edition, mandate the use of series commas in all cases. Regardless of the style you use, sometimes a sentence simply doesn't make sense, or seems to have multiple meanings, without the series comma.*

For example, in the sentence Our friends are mainly opera, classical music and ballet and theater fans, *it's hard to tell what the categories of fans are. They could be* opera, classical music and ballet, and theater fans, *or they could be* opera, classical music, and ballet and theater fans.

Even AP style advises writers to use a series comma "if an integral element of the series requires a conjunction: I had juice, toast, and ham and eggs for breakfast.*"*

You don't want the reader to have to go over something twice. A series comma allows you to pack more ideas into a sentence, to layer meaning.

Even if you don't normally use series commas, add them (or other punctuation) as necessary to the following sentences to clarify the meaning, or else reorder a series of elements to avoid ambiguity.

1. The flooding was worst at the point where New Jersey New York and Pennsylvania meet.

2. The company offers services from conceptualizing writing designing and producing spinoff pieces to locating better paper sources.

3. Scientists spotted large numbers of dolphins nurse and great white sharks and blue gray and humpback whales near the offshore station.

4. We help you identify your best customers market more effectively to current advertisers and subscribers and identify new product opportunities.

5. Theater news is constantly fresh with cast changes openings and closings finances and insider gossip endlessly fascinating to buffs.

Continued on next page

6. Jackets of every description fabric leather and fur were available at the bazaar.

7. The council is barred from dealing with foreign policy external security or issues that were left for diplomatic talks.

8. The commission has been talking to officials on all sides of the Northern Ireland peace effort the Irish and British governments Sinn Fein the political arm of the IRA and Protestant and Roman Catholic political leaders.

9. European employers complain that hiring employees costs them too much in health social security and vacation benefits.

10. The magazine features celebrity profiles fashion health and beauty stories relationship advice and cultural pieces on music family and food.

Answers are on page 76.

2-7. Semicolons in a Series

In general, a semicolon is used to separate items in a series when they have internal punctuation. Otherwise, commas are favored, even with a series of clauses. Commas may also be preferable in a straightforward sentence in which the elements are relatively short and only one has internal punctuation, especially if the internal punctuation appears in the last part of the series.

Add semicolons where you think they're appropriate in the following sentences.

1. The board's at-large members represent the four regions: Terry Smith, Rochester, NY, Chris Adler, Superior, WI, Kim Young, Chimayo, NM, and Pat Golden, Tallahassee, FL.

2. Marilyn Hacker's books include *Presentation Piece* (1974), which received the National Book Award, *Assumptions* (1985), the verse novel *Love, Death, and the Changing of the Seasons* (1990), and *Going Back to the River* (1990).

3. Because he loved to read, to write, and to edit, Mr. Diamond was considering a career in library work, marketing, or publishing.

4. Among the national programs sponsored by the Academy of American Poets are the Tanning Prize, the largest annual literary award in the country, the Atlas Fund, which provides financial assistance to non-commercial publishers of poetry, the Walt Whitman Award, and poetry prizes at 150 colleges and universities.

5. With the new spreadsheet program, you can add records, rename the labels assigned to fields, search your databases according to your own criteria, and change the names, length, or type of existing fields and the order in which the fields are listed.

6. The principal cites the school's record proudly: "Our test scores have been rising, almost 90 percent of our graduates go on to higher education, and we continue to launch new ideas to make the school stronger."

7. Arrange the eggplant slices in a shallow casserole dish that has been lightly coated with nonstick cooking spray, scatter the sliced onions, garlic, and celery over the top and in the spaces, pour the prepared tomato sauce over all, and bake at 350 degrees for 35 minutes.

8. The research summary highlights four areas of interest identified by the foundation: female adolescent development, debates in the research literature, research specific to girls of color, lesbian girls, and girls with disabilities, and images of girls in the media and popular culture.

9. Most previous studies have focused exclusively on factors that place adolescent girls at risk for such problems as depression, eating disorders, substance abuse, dropping out of school, and early childbearing.

Answers are on page 79.

2-8.   Commas, Colons, and Semicolons

When to use colons and semicolons instead of commas is often a problem. The "comma splice" (independent clauses joined by a comma) and overuse of the colon are frequent errors. Correct the punctuation in the following sentences by replacing commas with colons or semicolons or by deleting unnecessary colons.

1. You'll have to forgive my delay in replying, I've been working under a tight deadline this week.

2. He has only one ambition, to produce a Broadway musical.

3. Blue jeans are fashionable all over the world, however, Americans, the creators of this style, still wear jeans more often than the people of any other nation.

4. On my wish list to visit are Nashville, Mount Kisco and Pound Ridge, New York, San Francisco, and Santa Fe.

5. If you drop by the medical center without an appointment, you can be sure of one thing, an icy reception.

6. Present at the meeting were Mr. Connel, the president of ABC Company, Ms. Michaels and Ms. Roberts, the coordinators of the advertising campaign, Ms. Becker, the client, and Mr. Lupo, Ms. Becker's assistant.

7. The weather report predicted high winds, freezing rain, and snow, the highway patrol advised caution when driving, yet the storm blew out to sea.

8. The winner had a choice of one of three prizes, a trip around the world, a vacation home in the Bahamas, or a new car.

9. The governor issued this statement, "I have done nothing wrong, the IRS will find that my returns are all in order."

10. Many scientists share a similar view of our future, they believe that we have all the necessary technology to clean up the earth and restore nature's cycles.

11. Our order included: printer paper, mouse pads, monitor covers, and diskettes.

12. The cover design was created by: Matthew, Susan, and Fay, our graphic artists.

Answers are on page 80.

2-9. Em Dashes, Parentheses, or Commas— How to Choose?

When faced with a choice among em dashes (—), parentheses, and commas, many people ask the following questions: "Why did you use em dashes? I would have put that stuff in parentheses because it doesn't seem essential to the sentence." "Commas? You've got to be kidding! My supervisor would make me use em dashes. The trend is away from commas, isn't it?" "Isn't there a rule saying that em dashes should never be used in formal writing? We're not allowed to use them in our office."

There isn't one right—or simple—answer to these questions. However, the following three basic rules can be helpful in judging whether material has been set off appropriately.

Remember that setting off a group of words can either highlight it or relegate it to secondary importance. You could justify using a pair of em dashes, commas, or parentheses in almost all these sentences, but try to follow these rules:

- Use em dashes to emphasize information. Em dashes tell the reader, "Stop! Read this; it's really important." Also use em dashes to set off a series that already has internal commas.

- Use parentheses to deemphasize information. Parentheses tell the reader, "If you want to skip this stuff, go ahead; it's not all that important."

Continued on next page

- Use commas to show that information goes with the flow of the sentence. Commas tell the reader, "This information is as important as everything else in this sentence."

In many cases, emphasis is a matter of opinion, but sometimes one form of punctuation is preferable because of the flow or complexity of the sentence. Add em dashes, parentheses, or commas to help the reader understand the following sentences, which were adapted from Overcoming the 7 Devils That Ruin Success, *by James Dillehay (Torreon, NM: Warm Snow Publishers, 1994).*

1. By overcoming the seven devils that ruin success false success, fear of change, guilt, vanity, impatience, habit, and the clock author James Dillehay turned his life on a new path.

2. James Dillehay's father had painstakingly built the business an accomplishment that reflected a steady vision of success.

3. Adnan Sarhan the man who became Dillehay's teacher was born with a heritage of Sufi experiential knowledge and grew up in a cultural tradition where everyday life and spiritual development were interwoven.

4. The work of Sufi Master Adnan Sarhan director of the Sufi Foundation of America develops higher intelligence and awareness through a wide range of techniques exercises, meditation, drumming, movement, dancing, and whirling that heighten concentration.

5. Conflicting desires one for financial security, the other to study with Adnan often waged war in Dillehay's troubled brain.

6. Dillehay chose to follow the path of the Sufi the path that offered no promises the path that would force Dillehay to be the maker of his own destiny.

7. Dillehay claims that the second devil fear of change can be overcome only when someone's desire to change is stronger than the desire to stay stuck.

8. Impatience rushing to complete an activity before its natural time creates stress which in turn creates more impatience.

9. Sometimes we get so wrapped up in something our job, our family, a relationship that we forget about ourselves.

10. After the first day of the workshop December 4, 1994, the participants cleared their thoughts and felt a sense of readiness.

Answers are on page 83.

How Parentheses Are Used in Technical Documents

In technical documents, parentheses can be used to elaborate on or to clarify information. They can

- **Show acronyms or abbreviations:** A material balance area (MBA) can encompass one or more rooms.
- **Reference figures, chapters, and tables:** The XYZ system consists of four subsystems (see Fig. 3).
- **Make a qualifying statement:** They can be sorted by location (useful for taking a physical inventory) or other parameter.
- **State an exception:** The diagram delineates eight unit processes (not counting the vault) and denotes the process in which each step occurs.
- **Give equivalent units of measure:** The 111-km^2 (27,500-acre) park is adjacent to the communities of Los Alamos and White Rock.
- **Provide explanatory information that might otherwise go in a footnote:** The operating parameters (the information required to interface with the instrument and calculate the measured value) are stored in a partial record.
- **Show statistical information:** Performance statistics over a 1-year period show that the operating balances have an average accuracy of 0.060 g (1 σ).
- **State physics terminology:** Samples with large amounts of (α,n) emitters present special measurement problems.
- **Present mathematical expressions:** The rotation can be expressed as $2(x^2) + x - (1/x)$.
- **Give Latin names of species:** The most common tree is the one-seed juniper (*Juniperus monosperma*).

2-10. Punctuation with Quotation Marks

Here are the three basic rules for closing quotation marks. They apply to full and single quotation marks alike.

1. Commas and periods are placed inside closing quotation marks.

2. Colons and semicolons are placed outside closing quotation marks.

3. Question marks and exclamation points can be placed inside or outside closing quotation marks, depending on the sentence.

In the sentences below, the parts that don't *involve quotation marks are punctuated correctly. With that in mind, add the appropriate quotation marks and related punctuation for the quotes themselves. Some of the capitalization should help you.*

1. My accountant said, The best information on this topic can be found in the article Everything You Need to Know About Property Taxes

2. The economics professor asked, Have you read the article The Intelligent Consumer Demands More

3. I know only one way to sing The Star-Spangled Banner lipsynching

4. On Monday I will conduct the seminar WordPerfect for Windows on Tuesday I will conduct Microsoft Word

5. Who yelled, Look out

6. Can you believe old Scrooge said, We'll have a party next week

7. When you saw your boss at the restaurant, did you actually say When will I get a raise

8. The checks we need are the ones marked Insufficient Funds the bank teller told the manager

Answers are on page 84.

2-11. Quotation Marks and More

Insert quotation marks, punctuation marks, and capitalization as needed.

1. Megan asked her swimming coach am I going to swim both freestyle and butterfly in Saturday's meet.

2. Megan asked her swimming coach if she was going to swim both freestyle and butterfly in Saturday's meet.

3. The question is will we have enough money to fund the campaign the way we want to.

4. Please do not say no until you have heard all the advantages.

5. Before he went on his way, he quickly replied no.

6. Have you read the excellent journal article about endangered species called Where Have All the Animals Gone.

7. Eva explained I was shocked when my boss Mr. Kreps said, because our company can no longer pay its bills, we are declaring bankruptcy.

8. Heidi commented this year volunteers are hard to find because there are so many working mothers.

9. Heidi commented that this year volunteers are hard to find because there are so many working mothers.

10. George Washington…commanded the sun and the moon to stand still, and they obeyed him. [A toast given by Ben Franklin at a dinner in Versailles]

11. The issue is simply one between the haves and the have-nots.

12. Before you leave Doug commented please complete the forms that my secretary has for you.

Continued on next page

13. I participated in a seminar called Stress on the Job; I did not participate in the one called The One-Minute Manager.

14. I learned only one lesson from the article Investing Wisely invest in something safe.

Answers are on page 85.

2-12. Possessives I

In general, when a word doesn't end with an s, add an apostrophe and an s to indicate possession. When a word ends with an s, you may simply add an apostrophe, but many guides, including The Chicago Manual of Style, *14th edition, add an apostrophe and an s to these words as well. (Remember that it's important to be consistent in whichever practice you decide on.)*

Try your hand at forming the possessive of the following:

1. homes of my sons-in-law

2. rivers of Arkansas

3. house of Jim and Joan (joint ownership)

4. research of the Ph.D.s

5. advertising of McGraw-Hill, Inc.

6. estimate of Fred the electrician

7. idea of anyone else

8. depositions of the witnesses

9. the upper level of the airport

10. the daughter of one of my friends

Answers are on page 88.

2-13.   Possessives II

Correct the following sentences by inserting an apostrophe or an apostrophe with an s, or rewrite to avoid awkwardness.

1. The tree surgeon could not save the white spruces limb.

2. The users manual for the new software package was so confusing that most consumers returned it to the company.

3. Windows intuitive commands make it easy for users to move from one application to another.

4. I will be in Hawaii on Mothers Day, in New Mexico on April Fools Day, and in California on Veterans Day.

5. Grover Cleveland was the peoples choice.

6. Each participant filled out the Readers Comment Form.

7. Now that he has his bachelors degree, he plans to get his masters, and possibly his doctorate.

8. The National Secretaries Conference will be held in Houston this year.

9. For appearance sake, the feuding vice presidents kept their differences to themselves during the monthly staff meeting.

10. My brothers-in-laws idea was to have the family reunion at a spa.

11. We have been invited to a holiday party at the Roths.

12. The telephone companys presidents idea was to offer discount rates to seniors.

Answers are on page 89.

2-14. The Possessive with Verbals

The question of when to use the possessive before a verbal form continues to puzzle writers. The rules and answers that follow are based on four books: The New York Public Library Writer's Guide to Style and Usage (NYPL)*; the* Harbrace College Handbook, *13th edition;* Words Into Type (WIT)*; and* The Gregg Reference Manual, *8th edition* (Gregg).

Although all these sources agree that the possessive should be used with a gerund but not with a participle, a gerund and a participle both use the –ing form and therefore look the same, despite the fact that they function differently. As WIT *says,*

> *In sentences…in which a phrase containing a noun or pronoun and a participle is used as the object of a preposition, the participle may be construed as a noun…and the preceding noun made a possessive, or it [the participle] may be construed as a modifier of the noun. The idea of possession is much stronger in some sentences than in others, and sometimes failure to use a possessive might give the sentence a meaning different from that intended.*

In the example WIT *offers,* I object to the woman's wearing pearls, *"'the woman wearing pearls' conveys a different thought from 'the woman's wearing pearls.'"*

Ultimately, then, it all comes down to a question of meaning: What's objectionable, the woman herself or the fact that she happens to be wearing pearls? If it's the former, no possessive is required. If it's the latter, it takes the possessive to make the meaning clear. In other words, if the emphasis is on the noun, no possessive is used. If the emphasis is on the phrase or the thought, the possessive is used. Sometimes this distinction becomes clear only when you test it by juxtaposing a possessive against a noun as in the woman/woman's *example above.*

However, NYPL, WIT, *and* Gregg *all note that a sentence that sounds awkward should be revised, even if the possessive is grammatically correct. Here's an example from* WIT*:*

> I tried to prevent the boy's falling off the ladder.
> I tried to prevent the boy from falling off the ladder.

A rewrite can cause a slight shift in meaning, but sometimes it's worth the trade-off.

Decide which of the following sentences are correct as is (C), which require the possessive (P), and which would be better rewritten (R). The verbal form and the noun(s) it modifies are boldfaced.

1. Do you worry about **others copying** your ideas?

2. The new programs resulted in some **facilities submitting** to several inspections.

3. The university is involved in several efforts, including **faculty and students mentoring** young people.

4. When lack of investment would result in the proposed **service being** delayed, exceptions to the rules could become necessary.

5. Refusal to participate could result in the managed care **plan diverting** its patients to another group.

6. Some reasons for receiving this message include all **representatives being** busy.

7. The next technology will lead to even more **people having** access to the Web.

8. The success of our plan depends on **him being** alone.

9. The key to reducing the number of dog attacks is pet **owners** properly **training** their dogs.

Answers are on page 91.

2-1. Punctuation Grab Bag

1. Replace the question mark with a period.

   Why Yvonne Ryder left this agency so quickly has never been explained.

2. C

3. Eliminate the commas. The *who* clause is restrictive; therefore, no commas are needed to set it off.

   All employees who want to enroll for automatic deposit must complete the appropriate forms by the end of this month.

4. C

5. The conjunctive adverb *nevertheless* should be preceded by a semicolon.

   The supervisor of the graphics department is ill; nevertheless, the project was completed as scheduled.

   Or

   Create two sentences from one.

   The supervisor of the graphics department is ill. Nevertheless, the project was completed as scheduled.

6. C

7. The direct address of Ms. Conners requires that her name be set off by commas.

   The senior managers have requested that you, Ms. Conners, be in charge of the new resources library.

2-2. Help Stop Comma Litter

1. Commas should be placed before and after the year in a three-part date, but not between the month and year in a two-part date. When European or military style is used, no commas are needed: *6 June 1944*.

    The seminars will be conducted every Saturday from August 1, 1998, until November 30, 1998, at the town hall; certificates will be mailed in January 1999.

2. This sentence begins with a dependent clause (*Because...deadline*) and ends with an independent clause (*we...crunch*). A comma follows the dependent clause; if these two clauses were reversed, no comma would be needed because the dependent clause is restrictive. However, some dependent clauses—for example, those beginning with *although*—are always parenthetical and thus are always preceded by a comma.

    Because we must meet our Friday deadline, we have hired temporary employees to get us through the "crunch."

3. Traditionally, commas set off *Jr.* and *Sr., II* and *III,* and so on. Journalistic styles long ago abandoned this sort of comma, and *The Chicago Manual of Style*, 14th edition, has done so as well. The important point to remember is, if you decide to set off *Jr., Sr., II,* or *III,* don't forget the second comma.

    My father, Robert Smith III, and my grandfather, Robert Smith Jr., have both decided to toss their hats into the political arena.

    Or

    My father, Robert Smith, III, and my grandfather, Robert Smith, Jr., have both decided to toss their hats into the political arena.

4. No commas are used before and after the quotation because it's an appositive (that is, the same as the subject, *the wisecrack*). A quotation that's used as a subject, predicate noun, or restrictive appositive isn't set off by commas. (Commas would signify that the quotation wasn't essential to the sentence and could be lifted out.)

    The wisecrack "Men seldom make passes at girls who wear glasses" is attributed to Dorothy Parker.

5. Commas are used after an introductory dependent clause and between long independent clauses joined by a coordinate conjunction (*and, but, for, nor, or, yet*). A comma may be omitted between short independent clauses.

Traffic in the area is usually congested, but since the new construction work has begun on the bridge into the city, rush hour has become a nightmare.

6. Commas are used between coordinate adjectives (adjectives that are of equal weight), but a comma isn't placed after *well-established* because the entire phrase *nonprofit organization* is being modified. To test whether a comma is necessary between two adjectives, reverse them or place *and* between them. If the sentence still makes sense, a comma is needed.

   Although I was offered a good position at a small, newly created, privately owned company, I chose to accept an offer from a large, well-known, well-established nonprofit organization.

7. Commas are used to set off clauses that are nonrestrictive (parenthetical or nonessential to the meaning of the sentence). If all the candidates have indeed received funds from local PACs, commas are needed because the information is parenthetical. If only some candidates have received PAC funds and they alone plan to saturate the airwaves, the commas should be omitted because the information is essential.

   The candidates, who received last-minute funds from local PACs for a media blitz, plan to saturate the airwaves before election day.

   Or

   The candidates who received last-minute funds from local PACs for a media blitz plan to saturate the airwaves before election day.

8. The pronoun *which* usually introduces a nonrestrictive clause, which must be set off with commas. There was only one bicycle, and it was stolen from the driveway where it had been left.

   The bicycle, which was left in the driveway, was stolen last night.

9. The pronoun *that* introduces a restrictive clause; therefore, a comma shouldn't be used. More than one bicycle was on the premises, but only the one left in the driveway was stolen.

   The bicycle that was left in the driveway was stolen last night.

10. A comma should not separate a subject (*recognizing your own weaknesses as well as your strengths*) from its verb (*will help*).

    Recognizing your own weaknesses as well as your strengths will help you advance in your career.

2-3. Punctuation with Conjunctions

1. In compound sentences, a comma is used between two main clauses—that is, clauses that are complete sentences—joined by a coordinating conjunction (*and, but, for, or, nor,* and *yet*), unless the clause before the conjunction is very short. The example sentence is correctly punctuated.

   As a young writer, Bella ghosted for several mystery writers, and she now feels that this "ghosting" was more valuable than anything she learned in the classroom.

2. No comma is needed to separate the parts of the compound predicate *ghosted* and *has always felt*.

   Bella ghosted for several mystery writers and has always felt that this "ghosting" was more valuable than anything she learned in the classroom.

3. A semicolon is placed before a conjunctive adverb that connects two main clauses, and a comma usually follows conjunctive adverbs like *furthermore, therefore, moreover, nevertheless, consequently, still, otherwise, besides, also, however,* or *accordingly*. A comma isn't needed after the conjunctive adverbs *hence, nor, then, thus,* and *so*. No comma is needed between the two parts of the compound predicate.

   A private investigation novel, by its very nature, requires some violence; however, the trick is to make the violence rational and thus advance the plot.

4. To ensure clarity in a series of three or more elements, many people follow a style that places a comma (called the "serial comma") before the conjunction that connects words, phrases, or clauses. No comma is used before the conjunction *or* that connects the adjectives *psychic* and *extraterrestrial*, however.

   Medical research oddities, political trivia, or reports of unusual psychic or extraterrestrial events can trigger the beginning of an idea.

5. Commas generally should not be placed after coordinating conjunctions, even when the conjunction appears at the beginning of a sentence.

   Sometimes an amateur sleuth becomes involved in a case at the request of a friend. Or maybe the sleuth is just naturally curious.

6. When one or both verbs in two independent clauses are imperative, a comma is usually placed between the clauses for clarity. If the clauses (especially the first one) are very short, however, the comma is optional. Determining what's short can be a matter of opinion, but the second sentence below doesn't need a comma.

Orient your reader to the locale, and use background to your advantage.

But

Orient your reader and use background to your advantage.

7. A comma should follow an introductory dependent clause. However, a comma is optional before a dependent clause at the end of the sentence. We use it in the example because the two clauses are relatively long, but the second sentence below doesn't need it.

Avoid creating a villain who is more interesting than the protagonist, because the plot will be lopsided.

But

Avoid creating a convoluted plot because the reader will be left behind.

8. A compound-complex sentence usually consists of two main (independent) clauses that are joined by a coordinating conjunction and one or more subordinate (dependent) clauses. To punctuate this kind of sentence, place a comma before the coordinating conjunction (here, the first *but*) and then punctuate each clause separately. Both halves of this sentence have the same pattern: a subordinate clause that begins with the subordinate conjunction *when* followed by a main clause. A comma is needed after each clause.

When we speak of something that did not exist before, we are referring to an *invention*, but when we speak of something that did exist before but was not known, we are referring to a *discovery*.

9. If the internal punctuation of either of two main clauses joined by a coordinating conjunction causes confusion, use a semicolon between the two sentences instead and either delete or keep the conjunction, depending on the flow. If you keep it, don't use a comma after it. Using the serial comma can often make such a construction clearer, as in the second example.

Continued on next page

We requested information on patent attorneys, qualifications for applying for a patent and the length of time for which a patent is valid; but information on royalties, patents in other countries and the history of the United States Patent Office was sent instead.

Or

We requested information on patent attorneys, qualifications for applying for a patent, and the length of time for which a patent is valid, but information on royalties, patents in other countries, and the history of the United States Patent Office was sent instead.

10. When an introductory subordinate clause modifies both main clauses of a compound-complex sentence, no comma is necessary between the two main clauses. It's iffy whether a comma should be placed after the relatively short introductory clause because individual definitions of "short" are, in fact, relative. Here, it's used for clarity. Also, *that is*, in the sense of *in other words*, is always followed by a comma.

After you are granted a patent, you may sell the rights to a manufacturer or you may license your rights; that is, you may allow a company to make or sell your invention in return for royalties.

11. No commas are necessary to separate phrases joined with correlative conjunctions (*either...or, neither...nor, not only...but also*).

It is legal not only to patent an invention but also to patent an improvement on an already existing device or machine.

12. Items in a series with reiterated *and*s don't require separation by commas. In this example, however, *hundreds* might be read as modifying the other nouns that follow *seats*. In addition, the comparison between hundreds of people aboard in comfort and a solitary windblown pilot is obscured by the ungainly string of *and*s. Here are a couple of possible solutions.

A modern jet, with its hundreds of comfortable seats (and movies and lavatories and kitchens), hardly compares with the Wright brothers' biplane, in which a single pilot lay on his stomach with the wind gusting all around him.

Or

A modern jet—which has hundreds of comfortable seats, as well as movies and lavatories and kitchens—hardly compares with the Wright brothers' biplane, in which a single pilot lay on his stomach with the wind gusting all around him.

2-4. Punctuating Restrictive/Nonrestrictive Elements

Boldface has been used to show the nonrestrictive or restrictive element discussed in the answer.

1. In this sentence, the information in the clause is nonessential (extra) information; therefore, *that* should be replaced with *which* and commas should be used.

    Until recently, the modern Olympic Games, **which were begun in Athens, Greece, in 1896**, were held during the last year of each Olympiad—a period of four years ending in a leap year.

2. The name *Pindar* is a restrictive appositive and should not be set off with commas, but because all winners received wreaths, the *who* clause is nonrestrictive.

    During the Golden Age of Greece, the great poet **Pindar** wrote odes in honor of the winners, **who were presented with a laurel or wild olive wreath**.

3. *Stadion* is the restrictive appositive for *Greek word*. The clause *which…meters* is the nonrestrictive modifier of *stadion*, and the appositive phrase *the length…footraces* is the nonrestrictive modifier of *190 meters*.

    Stadium is derived from the Greek word *stadion*, **which is a unit of measure equal to about 190 meters, the length of the first footraces**.

4. It can be difficult to decide what "essential" information is. Some people might say that the phrase *on penalty of death* is essential information; women weren't just sent home, they were executed. Another might say that understanding the concept of being "forbidden" doesn't hinge on knowing the penalty for disobedience. Extraneous information that makes important qualifications can still be considered nonrestrictive—that's what makes it hard to decide.

    Only free male citizens were permitted to participate in the games; women were forbidden, **on penalty of death**, to even see them.

Continued on next page

5. No commas should set off the clause *who...times* because it restricts the meaning to a specific sixth-century wrestler. (But set off the entire nonessential phrase *a wrestler...times*.)

   Milo, **a wrestler in the sixth century B.C. who won the wrestling crown six times**, has often been considered the greatest athlete of ancient times.

6. The participial phrase *added in 1924* restricts the meaning to a particular competition, so no commas are needed.

   The competition **added in 1924** included cold-weather sports and became known as the Winter Games.

7. *The dictator* is immediately followed by the restrictive appositive *Adolf Hitler*, so no commas are needed. In 1936 the world had more than one dictator. Although the phrase after *Jesse Owens* might seem to be essential information, an appositive (*a black American...*) following a proper name is almost always set off by commas, or in this case by a single comma.

   At the 1936 Olympic Games, the dictator **Adolf Hitler** refused to acknowledge the triumphs of Jesse Owens, **a black American sprinter and long jumper**.

8. Set off the participial phrase *organized...Coubertin* because there's only one International Olympic Committee. Change *that* to *which* because it introduces a nonrestrictive clause.

   The International Olympic Committee, **organized in 1894 by Baron de Coubertin**, governs the Games and works with the national committees, **which must avoid any commercial, religious, or political interference**.

9. The clause *who...Kerrigan* defines the noun *spectator*, and the participial phrase *holding...skate* defines the noun *man*. The nonrestrictive appositive *an Olympic hopeful* is set off with commas.

   The spectator **who was shooting a video of Nancy Kerrigan, an Olympic hopeful**, caught on tape a man **holding a club while watching Kerrigan skate**.

2-5. Commas with Compound Adjectives

One comma should be added to each sentence.

1. Here, *childhood* is an attributive, so it stays where it is and isn't preceded by a comma. In the next phrase, however, the tooth fairy could just as well be described as *beautiful and open-handed* or as *open-handed and beautiful*, so the modifiers are coordinate adjectives and take a comma. In the final clause, *first* is a number and so isn't followed by a comma.

   Somehow, Sandy was not persuaded by the widely held childhood belief in a beautiful, open-handed tooth fairy; that first little incisor never did get put under the pillow.

2. Here, you can construe *interior* as an attributive or look at *interior designer* as a compound noun. In neither case is a comma appropriate. Lee's staff, however, can be seen as *talented and long-suffering*, so this pair of modifiers deserves a comma. In the final part of the sentence, both adjectival phrases have numbers and so receive no commas.

   Lee, a hard-working interior designer with a talented, long-suffering staff, had to make the best of a bad situation while dealing with three work-related disasters in one exhausting week.

3. In this sentence, *well-known* and *cost-free* could be interchanged or joined by *and*, so they can take a comma; but *data* is an attributive, inseparable from *source*—no comma. *Most important*, a superlative, can't be switched with *new*; cumulative modifiers take no comma.

   The project managers relied on a well-known, cost-free data source as they outlined the report for their most important new client.

4. This comparative form needs a hyphen for clarity, but it takes no comma because the modifiers are cumulative: What kind of land? *Agricultural.* What kind of agricultural land? *Less-productive. Played-out* and *marginal* could be switched or joined by *and*, so they can take a comma. *Same* and *high* couldn't be switched or joined by *and*, so they get no comma.

   The question is this: Should less-productive agricultural land in played-out, marginal areas be taxed at the same high rate as fields that yield bumper crops?

Continued on next page

5. Remember that two simple adjectives are often fine without a comma; if in doubt, try one or both of the tests. Either way, the *salad* phrase calls out for a comma. But *nice juicy steak*, while it passes the *and* test, falls apart when we try to change the order. Some people might add the comma anyway, for consistency within the sentence; others might leave it out, especially considering the necessary comma before *darling*.

Go ahead and eat your nice juicy steak, darling; I'll be perfectly happy with a cool, crisp salad.

Or

Go ahead and eat your nice, juicy steak, darling; I'll be perfectly happy with a cool, crisp salad.

The moral of the story is that judgment is essential. Some cases are clear-cut and some aren't; some matter and some don't. Being careful doesn't necessarily mean obsessing over commas. It's perfectly fine to say occasionally, "This one is okay either way. I'm not going to worry about it." That's not shirking a decision; it's keeping your perspective.

2-6. Essential Series Commas

1. There's no possibility of ambiguity here.

   The flooding was worst at the point where New Jersey, New York and Pennsylvania meet.

2. Without the comma, the reader doesn't know whether *designing and producing spinoff pieces* is one step or two. When speaking, people might pause after *pieces*; therefore they're sometimes tempted to put a comma there, but it's unnecessary and incorrect.

   The company offers services from conceptualizing, writing, designing, and producing spinoff pieces to locating better paper sources.

3. In a series like this, with simple, compound, and complex elements, it helps the reader if the items are listed in ascending order of complexity. Thus, although there are internal commas (*blue, gray,...*), as well as commas between the elements, semicolons aren't necessary for clarity. They're technically correct and you can certainly use them, but they're not necessary.

Scientists spotted large numbers of dolphins, nurse and great white sharks, and blue, gray, and humpback whales near the offshore station.

4. In this sentence, where the two *and*s could confuse the reader, the serial comma, if not exactly essential, is certainly helpful. Most readers would continue right past the first *and* and have to stop and look at the sentence again.

   We help you identify your best customers, market more effectively to current advertisers and subscribers, and identify new product opportunities.

5. Without the comma, the reader could assume that *finances and insider gossip* is a single element that is *endlessly fascinating to buffs*.

   Theater news is constantly fresh, with cast changes, openings and closings, finances, and insider gossip endlessly fascinating to buffs.

6. Here, *fabric, leather and fur* is clear enough without the series comma, but the phrase itself, which is in apposition to *Jackets of every description*, is much clearer if set off by em dashes. These signal a much more definitive break than commas and tell the reader to sit up and take notice.

   Jackets of every description—fabric, leather and fur—were available at the bazaar.

7. As written, this sentence is elliptical and ambiguous. Simply adding a comma won't clarify it. One possible meaning is

   The council is barred from dealing with foreign policy or external security, issues that were left for diplomatic talks.

   Another possible solution is

   The council is barred from dealing with foreign policy or external security, or with other issues that were left for diplomatic talks.

   Again, the comma after *security* is there for clarity.

Continued on next page

8. This sentence also has several possible solutions: First, adding a colon before the items in the list is helpful. Then, moving the items around so that the complex one is last makes it possible for the reader to understand the relationship among the parts.

    The commission has been talking to officials on all sides of the Northern Ireland peace effort: the Irish and British governments, Protestant and Roman Catholic political leaders, and Sinn Fein, the political arm of the IRA.

    Or use semicolons for more definitive breaks than commas:

    The commission has been talking to officials on all sides of the Northern Ireland peace effort: the Irish and British governments; Sinn Fein, the political arm of the IRA; and Protestant and Roman Catholic political leaders.

    Another possible solution is to put the definition of Sinn Fein in parentheses:

    The commission has been talking to officials on all sides of the Northern Ireland peace effort: the Irish and British governments, Protestant and Roman Catholic political leaders, and Sinn Fein (the political arm of the IRA).

9. Again, there's no ambiguity. The adjectives *health, social security and vacation* all modify *benefits*.

    European employers complain that hiring employees costs them too much in health, social security and vacation benefits.

10. As it stands, a lot of information is packed into this sentence. First, although the series comma is certainly essential, it may not be enough to clarify the meaning. A first cut would read

    The magazine features celebrity profiles, advice on relationships, stories on fashion, health, and beauty, and cultural pieces on music, family, and food.

    You could also use semicolons:

    The magazine features celebrity profiles; advice on relationships; stories on fashion, health, and beauty; and cultural pieces on music, family, and food.

2-7. Semicolons in a Series

1. Semicolons are the usual approach, although some people would use commas throughout.

   The board's at-large members represent the four regions: Terry Smith, Rochester, NY; Chris Adler, Superior, WI; Kim Young, Chimayo, NM; and Pat Golden, Tallahassee, FL.

2. Except for the comma between the date and the nonrestrictive clause, semicolons are the most likely solution; some people might stick with commas on the grounds that the dates divide the elements sufficiently—as could be argued for the postal abbreviations in number 1.

   Marilyn Hacker's books include *Presentation Piece* **(1974), which received the National Book Award;** *Assumptions* **(1985); the verse novel** *Love, Death, and the Changing of the Seasons* **(1990); and** *Going Back to the River* **(1990).**

3. Each series is fine with commas.

   Because he loved to read, to write, and to edit, Mr. Diamond was considering a career in library work, marketing, or publishing.

4. Without semicolons, *the largest annual literary award in the country* would be ambiguous.

   Among the national programs sponsored by the Academy of American Poets are the Tanning Prize, the largest annual literary award in the country; the Atlas Fund, which provides financial assistance to noncommercial publishers of poetry; the Walt Whitman Award; and poetry prizes at 150 colleges and universities.

5. Semicolons may seem superfluous until the final element in the series, but if you decide you need one for clarity there, you must use semicolons to separate the other items in the series.

   With the new spreadsheet program, you can add records; rename the labels assigned to fields; search your databases according to your own criteria; and change the names, length, or type of existing fields and the order in which the fields are listed.

6. Even though this is a series of independent clauses, most people would say that commas are fine here; semicolons could be used for a more formal tone.

Continued on next page

The principal cites the school's record proudly: "Our test scores have been rising, almost 90 percent of our graduates go on to higher education, and we continue to launch new ideas to make the school stronger."

7. If semicolons seem too stuffy for a recipe, break the instructions into two or more sentences.

Arrange the eggplant slices in a shallow casserole dish that has been lightly coated with nonstick cooking spray; scatter the sliced onions, garlic, and celery over the top and in the spaces; pour the prepared tomato sauce over all; and bake at 350 degrees for 35 minutes.

8. Semicolons are required because the third item has internal punctuation and is long, as well.

The research summary highlights four areas of interest identified by the foundation: female adolescent development; debates in the research literature; research specific to girls of color, lesbian girls, and girls with disabilities; and images of girls in the media and popular culture.

9. This one is fine with commas.

Most previous studies have focused exclusively on factors that place adolescent girls at risk for such problems as depression, eating disorders, substance abuse, dropping out of school, and early childbearing.

2-8. Commas, Colons, and Semicolons

Here are general rules for using the semicolon and the colon:

A. Use a semicolon to separate two main clauses when no coordinating conjunction (*and, for, or, nor, yet, but*) is used.

B. Use a semicolon to separate main clauses connected by a conjunctive adverb (*however, therefore, thus, nevertheless, moreover, consequently, nevertheless, otherwise,* and so on).

C. Use semicolons to separate a series of complex clauses or a series of grammatically equal items if the series is long or contains internal commas. Use semicolons in these cases even if the clauses or items are joined by a coordinating conjunction.

D. Use a colon to introduce a concluding explanation, a long or formal quotation, a series following a complete sentence, or an appositive (a noun or noun phrase placed beside another that it equals and explains). A colon should not be placed between a verb or a preposition and its object.

E. Use a colon to separate two main clauses when the second explains or amplifies the first.

Here's how rules A through E apply to the test sentences.

1. Rule A or E. This is a good example of a case in which either a semicolon or a colon would be acceptable. Because the two main clauses are closely related, the semicolon is correct. If the writer intended to emphasize that the second sentence explains the first, the colon is correct.

   You'll have to forgive my delay in replying; I've been working under a tight deadline this week.

2. Rule D.

   He has only one ambition: to produce a Broadway musical.

3. Rule B.

   Blue jeans are fashionable all over the world; however, Americans, the creators of this style, still wear jeans more often than the people of any other nation.

4. Rule C. For the name of a well-known city, you can omit the state name, even if the series includes other city-state pairs.

   On my wish list to visit are Nashville; Mount Kisco and Pound Ridge, New York; San Francisco; and Santa Fe.

5. Rule D.

   If you drop by the medical center without an appointment, you can be sure of one thing: an icy reception.

Continued on next page

6. Rule C.

   Present at the meeting were Mr. Connel, the president of ABC Company; Ms. Michaels and Ms. Roberts, the coordinators of the advertising campaign; Ms. Becker, the client; and Mr. Lupo, Ms. Becker's assistant.

7. Rule C.

   The weather report predicted high winds, freezing rain, and snow; the highway patrol advised caution when driving; yet the storm blew out to sea.

8. Rule D.

   The winner had a choice of one of three prizes: a trip around the world, a vacation home in the Bahamas, or a new car.

9. Rules D and A.

   The governor issued this statement: "I have done nothing wrong; the IRS will find that my returns are all in order."

10. Rule E. Whether or not to capitalize the first word after a colon is a style issue. Some styles say that if the group of words following the colon isn't a complete sentence, don't capitalize the first word; if the group of words following the colon is a complete sentence, however, do capitalize it.

    Many scientists share a similar view of our future: They believe that we have all the necessary technology to clean up the earth and restore nature's cycles.

11. Rule D. Most authorities won't allow the colon to be placed after the verb even if the information following the verb is broken out into a list. However, *The Gregg Reference Manual*, 8th edition, does allow a colon in displayed lists.

    Our order included printer paper, mouse pads, monitor covers, and diskettes.

12. Rule D. Neither a comma nor a colon should be used to separate a preposition from its object; therefore, deleting the colon after *by* makes this sentence correct. (The use of the serial comma is also a style decision.)

    The cover design was created by Matthew, Susan, and Fay, our graphic artists.

2-9. Em Dashes, Parentheses, or Commas— How to Choose?

In the context of a real document, the meaning would dictate the choice of punctuation. Here are some possible interpretations.

1. By overcoming the seven devils that ruin success—false success, fear of change, guilt, vanity, impatience, habit, and the clock— author James Dillehay turned his life on a new path.

2. James Dillehay's father had painstakingly built the business—an accomplishment that reflected a steady vision of success.

3. Adnan Sarhan, the man who became Dillehay's teacher, was born with a heritage of Sufi experiential knowledge and grew up in a cultural tradition where everyday life and spiritual development were interwoven.

4. The work of Sufi Master Adnan Sarhan, director of the Sufi Foundation of America, develops higher intelligence and aware- ness through a wide range of techniques (exercises, meditation, drumming, movement, dancing, and whirling) that heighten concentration.

5. Conflicting desires—one for financial security, the other to study with Adnan—often waged war in Dillehay's troubled brain.

6. Dillehay chose to follow the path of the Sufi, the path that offered no promises, the path that would force Dillehay to be the maker of his own destiny.

7. Dillehay claims that the second devil, fear of change, can be over- come only when someone's desire to change is stronger than the desire to stay stuck.

8. Impatience (rushing to complete an activity before its natural time) creates stress, which in turn creates more impatience.

9. Sometimes we get so wrapped up in something (our job, our family, a relationship) that we forget about ourselves.

10. After the first day of the workshop (December 4, 1994), the participants cleared their thoughts and felt a sense of readiness.

2-10. Punctuation with Quotation Marks

1. Follow rule 1. A quotation that falls within a quotation is set off with single quotation marks. No space is placed between single and double quotations. The placement of the period inside the closing quotation marks is an American usage, although in commands, the period might be placed outside the closing quotation mark, as in this example: *In sentence three of paragraph two, change "Monday" to "Thursday"*. The period isn't part of the change or the command. In British usage, the period may be placed outside the closing quotation mark, depending on the meaning (and the order of usage of double and single quotation marks is the opposite of American style).

   My accountant said, "The best information on this topic can be found in the article 'Everything You Need to Know About Property Taxes.'"

2. Because the quoted information is a question, place the question mark inside the closing quotation mark. The title of the article is a statement, so place the question mark outside the closing single quotation mark.

   The economics professor asked, "Have you read the article 'The Intelligent Consumer Demands More'?"

3. Rule 2 requires that the colon be placed outside the closing quotation mark.

   I know only one way to sing "The Star-Spangled Banner": lipsynching.

4. Rule 2 requires that the semicolon be placed outside the closing quotation mark, but rule 1 requires that the period be placed inside the closing quotation mark. This is a good example of a case where it doesn't seem to make much sense to place the period inside the closing quotation mark, but American usage punctuates this way.

   On Monday I will conduct the seminar "WordPerfect for Windows"; on Tuesday I will conduct "Microsoft Word."

5. According to *Words Into Type*, "If a question or exclamation occurs within a question, both ending at the same time, retain the stronger mark. It is often hard to say which is the stronger mark...." Here the exclamation is stronger.

   Who yelled, "Look out!"

6. The entire sentence is a question, and the quoted information is a statement; the question mark is placed outside the closing quotation mark. According to *Words Into Type*, if an exclamatory or an interrogative sentence ends at the same time as a statement, retain the exclamation point or the question mark and omit the period.★

   Can you believe old Scrooge said, "We'll have a party next week"?

7. Both the sentence and the quoted information are questions. According to *The Gregg Reference Manual*, 8th edition, a sentence can't end with two terminal marks of punctuation; the one used first is retained. Therefore, the question mark is placed inside the closing quotation mark.

   When you saw your boss at the restaurant, did you actually say, "When will I get a raise?"

8. Follow rule 1; place a comma inside the closing quotation marks.

   "The checks we need are the ones marked 'Insufficient Funds,'" the bank teller told the manager.

★The same advice against duplicate punctuation applies to punctuation in citing sources: If an article in quotation marks ends with a question mark, delete the comma that normally would have followed: for example, Scott Petersen, "Replevin: Are Your Documents Safe?" *Manuscripts*, Fall 1993.

2-11. Quotation Marks and More

The following rule applies to examples 1, 5, 7, and 8 but isn't repeated below: When a quotation falls at the end of a sentence, precede it with a comma and capitalize the first word of the quotation.

1. Place a question mark inside the quotation mark when the question mark applies only to the quoted material. Place the question mark outside the quotation mark when the entire sentence is a question and the quoted material isn't.

   Megan asked her swimming coach, "Am I going to swim both freestyle and butterfly in Saturday's meet?"

Continued on next page

2. This sentence is an indirect quotation (a paraphrase) and thus require no quotation marks. Correct as is.

   Megan asked her swimming coach if she was going to swim both freestyle and butterfly in Saturday's meet.

3. When a direct question falls at the end of a sentence, start the question with a capital letter and precede it with a comma. Place a question mark at the end of the sentence.

   The question is, Will we have enough money to fund the campaign the way we want to?

4. Don't use quotation marks to set off the words *yes* and *no* unless you want to emphasize that these were someone's exact words. Correct as is.

   Please do not say no until you have heard all the advantages.

5. Use quotation marks because *no* is a direct quotation. Place the period inside the quotation mark. When dependent clauses such as *before he went on his way* appear at the beginning of a sentence, they are usually followed by a comma.

   Before he went on his way, he quickly replied, "No."

6. Place the title of an article in quotation marks. When both the sentence and the quoted material require a question mark at the end of the sentence, use only one mark, the one that comes first.

   Have you read the excellent journal article about endangered species called "Where Have All the Animals Gone?"

7. When one quotation is inside another, use single quotes immediately inside the double quotes with no space between them. *Mr. Kreps* is set off with commas because this is an appositive renaming *my boss*. (His name is apparently nonessential information.)

   Eva explained, "I was shocked when my boss, Mr. Kreps, said, 'Because our company can no longer pay its bills, we are declaring bankruptcy.'"

8. Again, a period goes inside the quotation mark.

   Heidi commented, "This year volunteers are hard to find because there are so many working mothers."

9. This is another paraphrase that needs no quotation marks. Correct as is.

   Heidi commented that this year volunteers are hard to find because there are so many working mothers.

10. A quotation containing an ellipsis is a continuous quote even though some words have been omitted. Don't place quotation marks before or after the ellipsis.

    "George Washington...commanded the sun and the moon to stand still, and they obeyed him."

11. Don't use quotation marks around words or phrases taken from other parts of speech that are now well-established nouns—for example, *ifs, ands, or buts* and *pros and cons*. Correct as is.

    The issue is simply one between the haves and the have-nots.

12. When a direct quotation is interrupted by an expression like *he said* or *he commented*, place a comma and a closing quotation mark before the interrupting expression. Always place the comma inside the quotation mark, and place a comma after the verb that introduces the rest of the quote. Then put a beginning quotation mark before the continuation and an ending quote after the period. (The word *please* isn't capitalized here because it's a continuation of the first part of the quote.)

    "Before you leave," Doug commented, "please complete the forms that my secretary has for you."

13. Place seminar titles in quotations. A semicolon belongs outside the quotation mark. A comma is unnecessary after the word *called* because the title is restrictive information.

    I participated in a seminar called "Stress on the Job"; I did not participate in the one called "The One-Minute Manager."

14. A colon belongs outside the quotation mark. Capitalization of the first word after the colon is a matter of style. Some styles capitalize the first word after a colon, whether or not the word group is a complete sentence; other styles never capitalize the first word after a colon.

    I learned only one lesson from to the article "Investing Wisely": invest in something safe.

2-12. Possessives I

1. **my sons-in-law's homes** (To avoid awkwardness, it might be best to leave the phrase in its original form.)

2. **Arkansas' rivers** *or* **Arkansas's rivers** (Follow your style guide.)

3. **Jim and Joan's house** (To indicate joint ownership, add an apostrophe and *s* to the second name only.)

4. **the Ph.D.s' research**

5. **McGraw-Hill, Inc.'s advertising** (To form the possessive of a company or personal name that ends with an abbreviation, add an apostrophe and an *s* to the last part of the name, and drop the comma that normally follows *Inc., Jr., Sr., III,* etc.)

6. **Fred the electrician's estimate** (When a noun that would ordinarily be in the possessive is followed by a restrictive appositive—here, *the electrician*—add an apostrophe and an *s* to the appositive only.)

7. **anyone else's idea**

8. **witnesses' depositions**

9. **the airport's upper level** (Traditionally, nouns that referred to inanimate objects weren't supposed to be in the possessive, but this usage is transitional; most authorities no longer oppose it because no one would ever think that an airport "owns" the upper level.)

10. **the daughter of one of my friends** (No apostrophe is added to the *of* phrase here. The phrase *one of my friends' daughter* is not correct.)

2-13. Possessives II

1. Some people claim that the possessive shouldn't be used with inanimate objects because they can't show ownership. Others disagree, arguing that the alternative is unnecessary wordiness: *the white spruce's limb* versus *the limb of the white spruce.*

   In phrases relating to time and money, however, the possessive has always been acceptable: *this evening's storm, dawn's early light, five days' leave, three years' salary, six dollars' worth, Seven Years' War.*

   The tree surgeon could not save the white spruce's limb.

2. *User's manual* seems to be the current preference, although some guides are titled *users manual.* This usage will no doubt continue to evolve. However, no apostrophe is necessary with a descriptive word that simply ends in an *s*, such as *veterans groups.* This expression doesn't really indicate possession, but rather means "a group for [or of] veterans."

   The user's manual for the new software package was so confusing that most consumers returned it to the company.

3. Some people hold to tradition and place an *'s* at the end of all singular nouns, whether or not the noun ends in an *s.* The addition of the *'s* is a style decision and depends on how the word is pronounced: If a new syllable is created when the possessive is formed, an *'s* is usually added (*the boss's decision, Congress's recess*); if the addition of another syllable would make the word difficult to pronounce, only an apostrophe is added, as in this test example.

   Windows' intuitive commands make it easy for users to move from one application to another.

4. Names of holidays containing a possessive are usually singular—*Valentine's Day, Father's Day, New Year's Day, Martin Luther King's Birthday.* However, some are plural by tradition—*April Fools' Day;* some are true plurals—*Presidents' Day* is for Lincoln and Washington; and some have no apostrophe at all—*Veterans Day.*

   I will be in Hawaii on Mother's Day, in New Mexico on April Fools' Day, and in California on Veterans Day.

Continued on next page

5. The possessive of *people*, a collective noun that's plural in meaning, often causes difficulty; the possessive is formed by adding *'s*. *People* also has another plural form—*peoples*—that refers to groups united by a common heritage or culture: *The Ottoman Empire was made up of many nations and peoples*. Should a possessive be required for this form, it would be *peoples'*. This usage is uncommon, however, and the possessive even more so.

Grover Cleveland was the people's choice.

6. No apostrophe is necessary since *Readers* is being used as an adjective.

Each participant filled out the Readers Comment Form.

7. The singular possessive is used for *bachelor's* and *master's* because a degree is earned by one person. The word *master's* is the informal usage for "master's degree."

Now that he has his bachelor's degree, he plans to get his master's, and possibly his doctorate.

8. The apostrophe is often omitted in names and titles when the sense is more descriptive than possessive, that is, when *for* is meant rather than *of*. Usage is, however, idiosyncratic. Check exact names—*Teachers College*, but *Governors' Conference*.

The National Secretaries Conference will be held in Houston this year.

9. Certain expressions that end in *s* or the *s* sound traditionally take an apostrophe only—for *conscience'* and *righteousness' sake*. (Yes, it looks odd, but most style manuals agree with this usage.)

For appearance' sake, the feuding vice presidents kept their differences to themselves during the monthly staff meeting.

10. If a hyphenated compound is singular, add *'s* to the last element of the expression: *brother-in-law's idea*. If the compound is plural, as it is in this example, it's often best to avoid confusion by rewriting the sentence: *The idea that my brothers-in-law had....*

My brothers-in-law's idea was to have the family reunion at a spa.

11. The word *house* is understood; the house belongs to the Roths (plural), so the possessive is plural.

We have been invited to a holiday party at the Roths'.

12. Although grammatically correct, this sentence is awkward: A possessive modifying a possessive forces the reader to stop in midsentence to try to figure out what the writer is trying to say. The best solution is to rewrite the sentence: *The telephone company's president conceived the idea of offering....*

The telephone **company's president's idea** was to offer discount rates to seniors.

2-14. The Possessive with Verbals

1. (P) The possessive is needed to make it clear that you're not worrying about others per se but about their copying your ideas.

   Do you worry about **others' copying** your ideas?

2. (P) (R) The same reasoning used in answer 1 applies here.

   The new programs resulted in some **facilities' submitting** to several inspections.

   But some rewriting would improve the sentence. An alternative:

   The new programs made it necessary for some **facilities to submit** to several inspections.

3. (P) This sentence needs the possessive, but, in addition, the faculty and students share the responsibility for the mentoring. *NYPL* says, "When two or more people jointly possess an item, the apostrophe is placed after the noun closest to the item."

   The university is involved in several efforts, including **faculty and students' mentoring** young people.

4. (P) (R) Here the gerund (*being*) is followed by a past participle (*delayed*).

   When lack of investment could result in the proposed **service's being** delayed, exceptions to the rules could become necessary.

   Although the possessive is correct here, it looks and sounds awkward. It might be better to recast the phrase to "in delaying the proposed service."

Continued on next page

5. (P) This refusal would result not in the diversion of the plan itself but of its patients.

   Refusal to participate could result in the managed care plan's diverting its patients to another group.

6. (P) (R) Again, the emphasis here isn't on the representatives, but on the fact that they're all busy.

   Some reasons for receiving this message include all representatives' being busy.

   A little rewriting improves this sentence, which mentions *some reasons* but gives only one:

   One reason for receiving this message is that all representatives are busy.

7. (P) (R) The access belongs to the people, so the possessive form is required.

   The next technology will lead to even more people's having access to the Web.

   But this sentence seems awkward as well. Rewriting produces a slight shift in meaning, which is offset by the smoother flow:

   The next technology will mean that even more people will have access to the Web.

8. (P) This is a classic example of the kind of sentence that requires the possessive for the meaning to be clear. Our plan doesn't depend on him but on his being alone.

   The success of our plan depends on his being alone.

9. (P) The possessive is needed here. To see why, substitute a pronoun for the noun in question (***their*** *training their dogs*, not ***them*** *training their dogs*):

   The key to reducing the number of dog attacks is pet owners' properly training their dogs.

CHAPTER 3

USAGE AND GRAMMAR

- What's the criteria for that job?

- There's alot of people that still believe in UFOs.

- Like you and I, he feels badly about it.

- How does the student outcome data compare to other schools in the district?

- "a gift that's been laying around for 12 years"—ad for Glenlivet scotch in the *Atlantic Monthly*

All these are examples of English as it is mangled daily, around the water cooler, over the airwaves, and in print. This chapter tackles these problems and more: subject–verb agreement, verb tenses, adverbs versus adjectives, precision in word choice, proper placement of modifiers, use of idioms, and distinctions among confusables.

3-1. Subject-Verb Agreement I

In theory, subject-verb agreement is simple: A singular subject requires a singular verb, and a plural subject, a plural verb. In reality, two problems complicate the matter: locating the subject and determining whether it's singular or plural. Determine the subject and choose the correct verb in each sentence.

1. What if none of our district's students (wins, win) the $5,000 scholarship?

2. The jury (was, were) finally excused by the judge and left the courthouse.

3. She is one of the few contributors who not only (donates, donate) money but also (offers, offer) time.

4. Some of the sailboats (was, were) destroyed by the hurricane.

5. Two-thirds of the correspondence (has, have) yet to be answered.

6. Two-thirds of the freshmen (lives, live) in dormitories.

7. A small percentage of our employees (works, work) in this state but (lives, live) in another state.

8. The prime concern (is, are) better health care policies.

9. Preparing income tax returns (takes, take) all my time during tax season.

10. What our client wants to know and what we want our client to know (conflicts, conflict) with what our attorney wants our client to know.

Answers are on page 123.

3-2. Subject-Verb Agreement II

Choose the correct form of the verb in parentheses.

1. Neither my new plan nor the committee's proposals (is, are) acceptable.

2. Neither of the proposals (was, were) acceptable.

3. A designer and two graphic artists (has, have) been commissioned to work on the project.

4. A designer as well as two graphic artists (has, have) been commissioned to work on the project.

5. Jessica Smith is one of the veterinarians who (donates, donate) time to the local animal shelter and (tends, tend) to wounded animals.

6. Being the oldest sibling in the family and knowing efficient ways of running a household (has, have) not always worked to my advantage.

7. One of the software programs that (creates, create) scatter plots and histograms (was, were) on sale last week.

8. Rags to Riches Investors, a firm that (claims, claim) to double clients' money within a year, (charges, charge) a $50 monthly service fee.

9. Whether the jury believes the defendant and whether the judge allows certain evidence (remains, remain) to be seen.

10. When the faculty (is, are) not teaching, (it is, they are) pursuing independent research projects.

11. What (appears, appear) to be pipe dreams (is, are) often profitable ideas.

12. The number of homeowners interested in planting trees (seems, seem) to decrease every year.

Answers are on page 125.

3-3.   Subject-Verb Agreement III

Choose the correct form of the verb in parentheses.

1.   Nelson is the officer who (directs, direct) traffic and (dances, dance) at the same time.

2.   Nelson is one of the officers who (directs, direct) traffic and (dances, dance) at the same time.

3.   Nelson is the only one of the officers who (directs, direct) traffic and (dances, dance) at the same time.

4.   Each of the candidates who (is, are) running for office (smiles, smile) too much and (says, say) too little.

5.   The candidate as well as all her volunteers (smiles, smile) too much and (says, say) too little.

6.   Neither the nurses nor the doctor (believes, believe) in miracles, but all of them (is, are) hoping for one.

7.   Neither of the doctors (believes, believe) in miracles, but, in these cases, both (is, are) hoping for one.

8.   Since some of the manuscript (is, are) ready for the printer, some of the pages (is, are) to arrive by Friday.

9.   The data for the project (requires, require) immediate attention because the media (wants, want) to disclose the findings.

10.   It is I, not they, who (is, am, are) responsible for conducting the survey.

Answers are on page 127.

3-4. Subject-Verb Agreement IV

Choose the correct form of the verb in parentheses.

1. Your decision about pay raises that (is, are) being deferred for six months (is, are) sure to win you no friends.

2. When half of the mailing list (was, were) checked, we discovered that half of the people no longer (lives, live) at the same address as five years ago.

3. Developing photographs (takes, take) an enormous amount of time and patience.

4. To copyedit and to proofread manuscripts (requires, require) patience and skill.

5. Although a number of managers (has, have) decided to avoid the confrontation, the number of assistant managers to accept the challenge (keeps, keep) increasing.

6. There (is, are) a bookcase with broken shelves, a desk with no drawers, and a computer with no printer in my new office.

7. Each of the students (knows, know) that 3 plus 3 (equals, equal) 6, that 16 minus 7 (is, are) 9, that 5 times 8 (comes, come) to 40, and that 81 divided by 9 (results, result) in 9.

8. That they will accept the terms of the new contracts (is, are) almost definite.

9. Whether the data (was, were) correct and whether the criteria (was, were) accurate (remains, remain) to be seen.

10. Whom the public (elects, elect) for the judiciary positions and which bond issues the voters (passes, pass) (causes, cause) the increase or decrease in taxes.

Answers are on page 129.

3-5. Subject-Verb Agreement That 'Sounds' Wrong

Fix the subject-verb agreement in these sentences by changing the incorrect verbs. Some sentences are correct as written, though they may not "sound" right until you identify the subject.

1. While heading one of the seven working groups that make up the association's task force on quality, Whitmore has earned a reputation for running efficient meetings.

2. The gaff-topsail catfish is one of several members of the catfish family that carries eggs in its mouth.

3. He had never quite recovered from his attack of pneumonia, and the sudden rise in temperature—one of the fierce heat waves that devastate New York in the summer—was simply too much for him.

4. Although job training has usually been addressed on the local level, it is one of the emerging new programs that entwines community service and national concerns.

5. Voting is one of the most important freedoms that is included in the Constitution.

6. The *Beverly* is the only one of the boats that are equipped with both a motor and a sail.

7. I'm not sure why, but a hovering hummingbird is one of the images that comes to me as I puzzle out how to resolve my newest staffing problem.

8. If you are not one of the members who has already paid this year's dues, please use the coupon on the back page and send your payment today.

9. At Sunday's graduation ceremonies, Lynne—who uses a wheelchair— will be the only one in her class who has never missed a day of school.

10. Known as program H–1B, it is one of the few approaches that allows foreign professionals to work legally in the United States while seeking permanent residence here.

11. One or more of the rules that explain subject-verb agreement are often misinterpreted.

Answers are on page 130.

Making Verbs Agree with Fractions and Percentages

Which governs whether a verb should be singular or plural, the subject or the nearest noun? "By 1992, 47 percent of the population was (were) living in urban centers." "One-third of the respondents was (were) employed in the private sector." Obviously the subjects of those sentences are *47 percent* and *one-third*, not *population* and *respondents*, which just happen to be next to the verbs but are objects of prepositions.

Do you make the verb agree with the word next to it because it sounds better, or do you make it agree with the subject regardless of how it sounds?

For questions about subject-verb agreement you need a book like *Words Into Type*, *Webster's Dictionary of English Usage*, or *The New York Public Library Writer's Guide to Style and Usage* (NYPL). All three say that a verb following a fraction or percentage—like a verb following *all of, any of,* or *some of*—should agree in number with the noun following *of*. *NYPL* gives the following examples:

Three-quarters of the apple *was* left uneaten.

Three-quarters of the employees *are* at a seminar today.

The same principle applies to the percentage in the second sentence at the beginning of this discussion. "One-third of the respondents *were* employed in the private sector." The first sentence is trickier. Does *population* take a singular or a plural verb? According to *NYPL*, "Collective nouns require singular verbs when the group is functioning as a unit and plural verbs when the individual members of the group are considered to be acting independently." The idea of individuals within the population isn't strong, so write, "By 1992, 47 percent of the population *was* living in urban centers." But for other

similar sentences, use *were*: "By 1992, 47 percent of the population *were* city dwellers" (or change *population* to *people*).

It's important to understand that the rule about fractions and percentages isn't based on making the verb agree with the preceding word. The distinction is between "a single mass that's part of a larger mass" and "a number of units that are part of a larger number of units."

Usage guides should be a part of every writer's and editor's library. Others include Fowler's *A Dictionary of Modern English Usage*, Bernstein's *The Careful Writer*, Follett's *Modern American Usage*, and Copperud's *American Usage and Style: The Consensus*. But for some usage questions there's no consensus to be found. If the guides disagree, you'll have to read their discussions and then use your own judgment.

3-6.   Will the Real Subject Please Stand Up?

As you try your hand with the following sentences, some of which are correct, remember that the number of a pronoun subject is determined by its antecedent, the word to which it refers—not necessarily the nearest noun.

1. She is the first office-holder in recent years who have been able to forge significant ties with both ethnic minorities and separatist leaders.

2. Relying almost wholly on a long-since-disproved theory, the author never mentions the intensive and well-documented scholarly study of the ruins that has taken place in the past 20 years.

3. An alternative to newsgroups are mailing lists.

4. His demonstrated leadership, deep community roots, and progressive stand on local issues makes him an attractive candidate for the County Board.

5. A trio of top bluegrass bands headlines the annual spring concert.

6. The professor outlined three reasons why training in speaking, reading, and acting are helpful in vocal improvement.

7. E-mail messages pass through a series of routers that direct them to their intended destinations.

8. The Women's Philharmonic, which made their East Coast debut in a recent performance, has a revolutionary goal—to change what is played in every concert hall by incorporating the work of women composers into the orchestral repertoire.

9. We propose a workshop approach for this project because the variation in individual goals and the need for group interaction requires integrated planning and evaluation.

10. If you asked me about the film version of the Pocahontas story, I'd say that Disney does entertainment, and they do it very well.

11. He argued that widespread prejudice and discrimination still exists, although greater inclusiveness in education and hiring have greatly benefited society as a whole.

12. The Pentagon and the Base Closing Commission have criteria that apply to each base.

Answers are on page 132.

3-7. The Subjunctive: Wishful Thinking?

The subjunctive mood. *It can be an intimidating term, even for those who bat it around occasionally at work.* Words Into Type *says that the subjunctive mood "is almost extinct in spoken English and is passing away in written English." Some grammarians call the subjunctive stodgy and prefer recasting the verb in the indicative mood, but others enjoy cultivating its proper use.*

There's room in the realm of usage for personal preference. And there are situations in which the subjunctive is still appropriate, chiefly to emphasize statements that are conditional rather than factual.

In forming the subjunctive mood the basic rules of tense are reversed: Present tense is used for past, past is used for present, and be *is used for* is, am, *and* are. *The sub-junctive mood is still widely used in three kinds of sentences:*

- Sentences with *that* clauses that express a suggestion, a demand, or a requirement:

  When any form of the verb *to be* appears in the dependent clause, the form *be* is used with all subjects. For verbs other than *to be*, the present tense is used for all subjects. An *s* is never added to the verb, even if the subject is singular. For example: I demand that he *see* to the arrangements.

- Sentences using the verb *to wish*:

  The verb in the dependent clause must be in the past tense to express what is desired at the present time. For the verb *to be*, use *were* with both singular and plural. For example: I wish he *were* here.

Continued on next page

- Sentences stating conditions that are improbable, doubtful, or contrary to fact:

The verb in the *if* clause (or the *as if* or *as though* clause) is in the past tense to express present time. To express past time, the verb in the *if* clause (or the *as if* or *as though* clause) is in the past perfect tense. For example: If I *were* you, I'd buy more stock. (present) If he *had spoken* up, he would have averted the crisis.

With these rules in mind, correct any errors in the following sentences by changing the indicative to the subjunctive or vice versa. Note that some sentences may be correct.

1. It's important that your mother remembers to anchor the boat.

2. "If I were the lifeguard, I would never fall asleep in my chair," Weber said.

3. "Jamal likes to wear black shoes. Be that as it may," Sandra said, "he needs to wear brown shoes with a brown suit."

4. If I were living on a 70-acre ranch, I would own 3 dogs, 12 chickens, and as many horses as the land would hold. But unless I find a bag of cash in the basement, I'll be living in this tiny house forever.

5. The rabbi asked that the congregation should sit.

6. Next I looked to see if the ground were clear.

7. If I was your boss instead of your sister, I'd fire you.

8. Anse wished bitterly that his son were there to see the new tractor.

9. Our handbook requires that acceptance letters be sent out within a week of application.

10. If stocks fall, much of executive pay would evaporate.

Answers are on page 134.

3-8. Verb Forms

Determining the correct forms of the past tense and past participles of some irregular English verbs isn't always easy. Give the correct forms for these verbs.

Present	Past	Past Participle
bear	_____	_____
beat	_____	_____
burst	_____	_____
creep	_____	_____
dive	_____	_____
drink	_____	_____
get	_____	_____
hang	_____	_____
lay	_____	_____
lead	_____	_____
lend	_____	_____
lie	_____	_____
prove	_____	_____
raise	_____	_____
rise	_____	_____
shine	_____	_____

Continued on next page

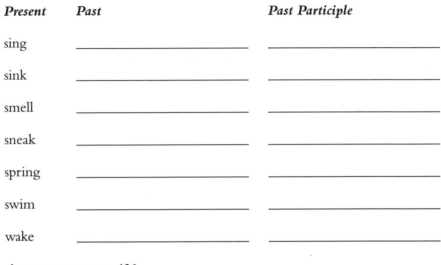

Present	Past	Past Participle
sing	_____	_____
sink	_____	_____
smell	_____	_____
sneak	_____	_____
spring	_____	_____
swim	_____	_____
wake	_____	_____

Answers are on page 136.

if/whether

Is there really a distinction between *whether* and *if*? Most authorities say there is. Theodore Bernstein in *The Careful Writer* says that *whether* is "the normal word used to introduce a noun clause." *Whether* should be used to introduce a noun clause serving as a subject: "Whether politicians can agree on a way to reduce crime is doubtful." But *if* can be and commonly is used interchangeably with *whether* to introduce noun clauses that follow verbs such as *ask,*

doubt, hear, learn, and *know.* Either word is acceptable in this sentence: "Do researchers know (if/whether) a virus causes the common cold?"

A note of caution: To avoid confusion, reserve *if* for expressing conditional statements ("If this is true, then that...."). "Tell me if I have spinach between my teeth" can have a conditional sense—"Should that ever be the case, tell me"—as well as a true-or-false sense: "In case that is true now, tell me." *Whether,* which implies

or not, is clearer in the true-or-false case.

By the way, saying *whether or not* is usually unnecessary, although it has been considered acceptable for more than 300 years. The one case where adding *or not* is required is with the use of *whether* to introduce a noun clause that functions as a sentence adverb: "Whether or not you agree with my opinions, I have the right to voice them."

3-9. Feeling Tense and Moody

Much writing involves future conditional sentences (If X happens, Y will result). *But many writers are wary of sounding too sure about an outcome, so they use* would *rather than* will. *Our ear tells us that when the main clause contains* would, *the subordinate clause needs to be in the past tense* (If X happened, Y would result). *The problem is that this rule is so often broken that everyone is beginning to have deep doubts about it. Is there anything wrong with the sequence of tenses in the following sentences? If so, correct the boldfaced verb.*

1. The rules would require that the Congress adjust tax schedules so that overall growth in real incomes **does** not push people into higher income tax brackets.

2. All Americans would suffer in some way if benefits for Social Security or Medicare **fall**.

3. If discretionary spending **is** frozen, the deficit would rise in 1997 and 1998 but would then begin to decline.

4. The accounts rely on the theory that existing capital would suffer a drop in value when an investment incentive **rises**, in the same way that a bond would if the interest rate **rises**.

5. The size of the future problem is so great that eliminating the deficit by 2002 would not alone ensure that future deficits **remain** at an acceptable level without additional changes in spending and taxes.

6. Even if such consumers could repay a loan out of their prospective earnings, lenders **may** not extend one because it could not be secured by a real asset.

Answers are on page 137.

3-10.   The Placement of Modifiers

To correct the problems with the placement of modifiers in the sentences that follow, you may need to add some words of your own. Remember that single adjectives are usually placed just before the words they modify. Adjective phrases and clauses are placed immediately after the words they modify, except when a phrase and a clause modify the same word; then the phrase precedes the clause. Adverb modifiers should be placed so that the meaning is expressed exactly.

1. The thieves were apprehended soon after the convenience store was robbed by the police.

2. While cooking for twelve people, the power went off because of the electrical storm.

3. Rushing to meet the Friday deadline, the manuscript did not get a final polishing by the editors.

4. The instructor told the participants when the seminar was over they would receive certificates.

5. To understand the proposal for the new training program completely, all the supervisors' recommendations should be reviewed by senior managers.

Fixing Misplaced Modifiers

- **A misplaced modifier** is a word, phrase, or clause that's been placed incorrectly in the sentence, thus distorting the meaning. A misplaced modifier can be ambiguous or downright funny.
- **A squinting modifier** is a word, phrase, or clause that may logically refer to either a preceding or following word and thus is ambiguous. First establish which word is being modified, then move the modifier.

- **A limiting modifier** is a word that should immediately precede the word, phrase, or clause that it refers to. Examples of limiting modifiers are *almost, exactly, hardly, just, merely, only, scarcely,* and *simply*. A common error is to place these modifiers before the verb, regardless of the word being modified.
- **A dangling modifier** is a phrase or an elliptical clause (a clause in which some essential words are omitted) that's placed next to a word it can't sensibly modify. Dangling modifiers are usually found at the beginning of sentences, and often the word that should be modified by the dangler has been dropped. Change the dangling phrase to a clause or move the word that should be modified to immediately follow the modifier.

6. The jogger saw the sailboats racing while running through the park.

7. People who exercise occasionally may have some minor aches and pains.

8. By installing an upgraded telephone system, every telephone line can be answered from anywhere in the office.

9. Everyone should have a dental checkup to keep teeth healthy at least twice a year.

Answers are on page 140.

3-11. Misplaced Modifiers

In the sentences below, move the misplaced modifier next to the word it actually modifies.

1. The teacher said that my son only did his homework on Wednesdays.

2. The coordinator of the adult education program told us eventually the institution would purchase new computers for the lab.

3. While adjusting his new field glasses, a red-headed woodpecker landed on a nearby branch.

4. On recalculating the tax return totals, the discrepancy between my accountant's results and the IRS's results became apparent.

5. When four years old, Kate's father was transferred to San Francisco to direct the marketing division.

6. He suggested that our 12-year-old start mowing the lawn last night.

7. Madeline showed the available flowers to the customer in the refrigerated showcase.

8. While the bank teller stood still grasping the money tightly the robber darted forward.

Answers are on page 141.

3-12. Shifty Adverbs

Decide where to place the adverb in parentheses to best advantage—for the sound of it and for best sense. That is, place it near the word in the sentence you wish to emphasize.

1. (foolishly) Hoping for good seats at the movie theater, we were tempted to drive faster.

2. (finally) We were glad to have pinpointed the problem.

3. (better) Will this software help us to achieve the graphic effects we want?

4. (at last) Our friend the acquisitions editor told us that he had found the manuscript that would make his career: *Collecting Cuban Cigars.*

5. (never) I'm telling the truth—I could have made something like that up in a million years.

6. (spontaneously) The art director can look at a page and think of better ways it could have been designed.

7. (more fully) Many editors type up a page-by-page query cover sheet that explains the marginal notes.

8. (unfortunately) This seems to be our only option.

9. (completely) If you plan to renovate the bathroom, you'll need a permit.

10. (only) He said that he loved me.

Answers are on page 142.

3-13. Adverb or Adjective? Confusion with -*ly* Words

Myth: *Words ending in –ly are always adverbs.*

Fact: *No word is a part of speech until it's used in a sentence.*

Remember to use an adverb only when an adverb is required to modify or explain the verb. Choose the correct answer in parentheses below and justify your choice.

1. She feels (bad, badly).

2. He was not hurt very (bad, badly) when he collided with another skater on the ice.

3. The bell sounded (loud, loudly).

4. He appeared (quiet, quietly).

5. He felt (careful, carefully) along the runner of the bobsled for any flaws.

Answers are on page 144.

Adverb or Adjective?

To decide whether to use an adverb or an adjective, remember that when the word that follows a verb modifies the subject (a noun or pronoun), an adjective is used. Also, an adjective usually follows any form of the verb *to be*, as well as the verbs *appear, sound, look, feel, taste, seem, become,* and *smell* when they're used as linking verbs, rather than as action verbs.

Here's an easy way to decide whether an adverb or an adjective is called for. If *is, are, was, were,* or some other form of the verb *to be* can be substituted for the verb, use the adjective:

They look *sad.*

When you substitute the word *are—They are sad—*the sentence makes sense, so the adjective *sad* is correct.

They looked *sadly* at the damage done by the tornado.

It doesn't make sense to substitute *are* here—*They are sadly at the damage done by the tornado*—so the adverb *sadly* is correct.

Another test: If the words *in a [adjective] manner* can be substituted for the -*ly* word, use an adverb. Remember that adverbs also can modify adjectives.

They took my advice *seriously.*

They took my advice in a serious manner, so *seriously* is correct.

Her plan is *real* good.

Literally, *her plan is in a real good manner,* which makes no sense—this is a common error.

3-14.   Pin Down Vague Terms of Measurement

Each of the statements below contains a subjective measurement or proportion open to misinterpretation. Isolate the ambiguity and identify the missing information needed to make the point clearer. In some cases, the measurement may not need to be more specific because detail isn't essential to the meaning of the sentence.

1. Virtually all the women at the seminar chose to attend the Macintosh design workshop rather than the IBM spreadsheet workshop.

2. Please have your manager answer this letter as soon as possible.

3. If you buy photocopier paper in bulk, we can offer you a substantial discount.

4. I've only asked you to work late a time or two lately.

5. High winds caused terrible destruction in the small community.

6. The candidate won by a slight majority.

7. For someone who's been at the newspaper for only a short while, you've made more than a few good contacts.

8. They drove at breakneck speed to the beach.

9. This project should require a minimal amount of effort from the staff.

Answers are on page 145.

---

more than/over

Despite a long battle by grammarians to preserve what is in effect the *fewer/less* distinction—between countable numbers and gross amounts—dictionaries, commentators, and many excellent writers no longer distinguish between *more than* and *over*.

Copperud tells us that Ambrose Bierce, in *Write It Right*, "an extremely idiosyncratic guide" (they don't make them any more), was the first to attempt to impose a rule on these terms. In cases where the distinction is logical and obvious, writers will, of course, be perfectly correct to use the *fewer/less* rule, as for statements such as "I have waited more than three days for you to return my phone message" and "It's been over a year since I heard from my niece in Louisiana."

But someone who happens to say "I waited over two hours for the doctor" or "We've lived here for more than a year" is also correct, by most lights, and not to be frowned on merely from ambrosial habit.

3-15. Precision in the Choice of Words

Everyone has mental blocks about certain word choices such as less/fewer *or* among/between. *The sentences below contain common errors in word choice. Find the errors and correct them, but make sure you substitute the precise word.*

1. Because Dale lives further from the convention center than I do, I will attend the conference.

2. After our company contracted with a new printer, our proofreader found less mistakes than usual.

3. Since I was anxious to buy a new car, I was thrilled with both my promotion and my raise.

4. The bonus money was divided evenly between the training, graphics, editing, and proofreading departments.

5. The client was disappointed with the printer because the newsletters were delivered late.

6. By next spring, everyone of the employees will be eligible to participate in the new training program.

7. To insure that our budget proposal is correct, our supervisor asked us to triple-check our figures.

8. Due to his poor health, Mr. Saltz decided to resign from his stressful job.

9. A large percent of registered voters went to the polls in inclement weather to support their candidates.

10. This report has laid untouched on my desk for three days.

Answers are on page 146.

3-16. More on Precise Words

Each of the following sentences contains a word that's used incorrectly. Can you find and correct the error?

1. The new corporation is comprised of five major divisions.

2. Although we have encountered many problems, it looks like we will meet the manager's unreasonable deadline.

3. After six long, grueling years, my son finally graduated Boston University.

4. The supervisor inferred in his pep talk that the publications department would receive a substantial bonus if the proposal was a success.

5. Of all the presentations about new software products, the ABC Company's was the most unique.

6. The word processing operators were disappointed in the new spell-check software because it did not highlight repeated words.

7. Rebecca, an inexperienced secretary, was so enamored with her boss that she thought he could do no wrong.

8. The clever hotel magnate managed to allude IRS scrutiny by falsifying his income tax forms.

9. The illustrator's ability to draw complimented the author's ability to tell a story.

10. Although the law partners were enemies on the tennis court, they always agreed on legal issues.

Answers are on page 147.

3-17. Using the Right Idiomatic Prepositions

According to Theodore Bernstein in The Careful Writer, *"The proper preposition is a matter of idiom; and idioms, if they do not come 'naturally,' must be either learned or looked up." He advises that "if a desired idiom cannot be found here [in his book] or in an unabridged dictionary..., the only thing to do is to consult three knowing friends and get a consensus."* Words Into Type *also offers a list of prepositional idioms. In the sentences below, decide whether the boldfaced prepositions and the words preceding them are used correctly. If not, correct the prepositions.*

1. The inexperienced teacher was **annoyed with** the poor conduct of the students.

2. Although Morton was **angry at** himself for overlooking such a blatant error, he decided to make the best of a bad situation.

3. **I concur with** the opinion that this company needs a reorganization of managerial responsibilities.

4. As an **advocate for** free speech, she supported the court's decision.

5. When she **parted with** her colleagues to take a new job, she was not sure whether she would ever see them again.

6. The students were so **preoccupied by** evaluating the results of the experiment that they didn't notice they were the only two left in the lab.

7. His **affinity for** open spaces forced him out of the megalopolis and into rural America.

8. Today's emphasis on plain English seems **analogous with** Franklin Roosevelt's belief that plain words reach more people.

9. **Compared to** last year's losses, this year's balance sheet looks promising.

Answers are on page 149.

3-18. More Right Prepositions

Decide whether the boldfaced prepositions and the words preceding them are used correctly. If not, correct the prepositions.

1. Because George was **careless about** his editing, he lost his job.

2. The manager was so **disgusted with** her supervisor's swearing that she asked for a transfer to another department.

3. The antique furniture presented a **contrast with** the high-tech architecture of the office building.

4. **Ranging between** 230 **and** 250 degrees, the oil bath was preferred to the water bath for the experiment.

5. Mr. Jacobs was unable to hide his **resentment at** his supervisor, Ms. Simmons, when she rejected his reorganization plan.

6. A substantive editor must be **attentive about** tone and readability, as well as **about** organization and content.

7. Being **well educated in** the field of civil engineering, Ms. Hogan was an excellent candidate for the position of department manager.

8. A believer in saving the environment, David was willing to **labor at** the recycling movement in his community.

9. The writer was **wary about** the inexperienced editor's being responsible for reorganizing the manuscript.

Answers are on page 150.

---

compare with/compare to

Webster's Dictionary of English Usage notes that *compare with* and *compare to*, particularly in the past tense, have become so interchangeable that the two no longer convey reliably distinctive meanings. The *Harper Dictionary of Contemporary Usage* recommends observing the distinction in formal speech and written communication but also observes that in informal speech the two prepositions have become interchangeable.

If the goal is to point out dissimilarities between persons, things, or objects, it's best to use *contrast with*: "The acid precision of Dorothy Parker's wit contrasts with Roseanne's slapstick comedy."

Maintaining Distinctions

In a commentary for the *Atlantic Monthly* (May 1995), Cullen Murphy described the confusion between *lie* and *lay* as an old and understandable problem:

Among other things, the verbs share a manifestation (*lay*). Moreover, when you *lay* something down, you cause it to *lie*. Also, there was once a reflexive pronominal use of *lay* (as in "Now I *lay* me down to sleep..."), which has undoubtedly sown confusion. And *lie* and *lay* as nouns, connoting a configuration of ground, can at times be used interchangeably ("the *lie* or *lay* of the land").

Still, he notes, the distinction between the two words was generally maintained over the past two centuries, until *lay* began to overtake *lie* not just in speech, but in formal writing in recent decades. In fact, Murphy attributes the growing acceptance of *lay* to the declining influence of the print media.

Does the apparent triumph of spoken over written English mean that we should give up on trying to maintain the distinctions between this and other confusables? Is the *lie/lay* distinction "fragile and impractical," as linguist Dwight Bolinger is said to argue? And if we give up on *lie/lay*, do we also throw in the towel on all the other confusables that our spell checker doesn't help us with?

Knowing the correct pronunciation can help writers avoid using *loathe* (hate) when they mean *loath* (reluctant), *loose* (not bound) when they mean *lose* (to experience loss), *suit* (apparel) when they mean *suite* (a grouping of furniture, rooms, or musical themes), and *prophecy* (noun) when they mean *prophesy* (verb). And using the preferred pronunciation for *route* (like *root*) can help differentiate this word (meaning a way for travel) from *rout* (an overwhelming defeat). But pronunciation doesn't help with *aid/aide, cite/site/sight, dual/duel, foreword/forward, forego/forgo, led/lead, principle/principal, pour/pore, palate/palette/pallet*, and similar land mines.

And how about those pesky apostrophes? We've all become accustomed to dropping the apostrophe in geographic names such as *Harpers Ferry* and *Hells Canyon*. Only the citizens of *Martha's Vineyard* have prevailed against the U.S. government geographers in this regard. And we might almost be willing to accept *childrens* if it meant we'd no longer see *her's* and *their's*, not to mention *potato's* and *bean's*.

But to accept *lay* for *lie* would be admitting only the nose of the camel among confusables. The *Random House Dictionary of the English Language, Second Edition, Unabridged* lists 115 sets of "Words Commonly Confused," of which here are only a few:

adapt:	to make fit
adopt:	to take as one's own
amend:	to modify
emend:	to edit or correct
corporal:	of the body
corporeal:	material, tangible
desert:	arid region; to leave or abandon
dessert:	final course of a meal (but note: "just deserts")
equable:	uniform
equitable:	fair
flounder:	to struggle awkwardly
founder:	to sink, fail
prescribe:	to recommend
proscribe:	to prohibit

To appreciate the scope of the problem more fully, consider the 84-page discussion of "Misused and Easily Confused Words" in *The New York Public Library Writer's Guide to Style and Usage*. And neither of those sources includes the commonly confused pair *degree/diploma*. (A high school graduate has earned a *diploma*.)

3-19. Second Cousin Exercise

In the following sentences, replace the not quite right, "second cousin" words with more accurate choices. **Note:** *These sentences weren't manufactured. All of them have appeared in print.*

1. He was the worst knitpicker I've ever seen.

2. The speaker placed her notes on the podium.

3. We should try to hone in on what the real problem is.

4. The editor carefully amended the text.

5. To prevent the enemy from importing missiles, the President ordered a boycott of the harbor.

6. He poured over the dusty manuscript for hours.

7. More importantly, the whole problem centered around a misunderstanding.

8. Joe tried to convince me to buy a 40-volume encyclopedia.

9. In his report, the engineer sighted several discreet examples of poor design practice.

Answers are on page 151.

Terms for Language Errors

Here are some common terms that describe erroneous grammatical constructions.

Ambiguity:	Construction with more than one possible meaning ("Mary told Jane her work was done.")
Malapropism:	Misapplication of words, especially by use of words that are similar in sound ("Illiterate him from your memory.")
Pleonasm:	Use of more words than needed to denote sense ("He walked the entire distance downtown on foot.")
Solecism:	Error in grammar or idiom ("between you and I")
Tautology:	Needless repetition of an idea, statement, or word ("widow woman," "a biography of his life")

3-20. *that* vs. *which* and *who*

Change the boldface which *to* that *or* who *in these sentences (or delete the word if possible) and indicate whether the clause is restrictive (essential) or nonrestrictive (nonessential).*

1. The team **which** is responsible for drafting the Strategic Alignment Policy Summary reports directly to the president.

2. The SAPS team **which** has been working overtime on the policy manual **which** is overdue sent out for pizza.

3. "Strategic alignment" **which** is a plan for a 50 percent reduction in force is key to doubling corporate income which has been steadily declining.

4. Corporate communicators often can't combat the rumors **which** circulate in the wake of management transitions.

5. Positions **which** are not key and **which** are left open because of disgruntled employees **which** retire early will not be filled.

6. Documents **which** were published by the Office of Technology Assessment **which** has been abolished are still available through the Superintendent of Documents, P.O. Box 371954, Pittsburgh, PA 15250-7974.

7. Portable Document Format (PDF) **which** is an almost exact replica of the printed product is one way **which** documents can be made available on the Internet.

8. The Institute for Federal Printing and Publishing is offering a service to its customers **which** elect to receive reminders of upcoming classes by fax.

9. A thorough procedure guide **which** has been prepared by Conference Call USA **which** is a provider of teleconferencing services explained to participants **which** wanted to retrieve printed materials how to use fax-on-demand.

Continued on next page

10. Memories of people, places, and things **which** meant a lot to my parents were carefully preserved in scrapbooks **which** we showed to the children on our last visit.

11. Downsizing the workforce **which** grew in the 1980s is a task **which** no company undertakes gladly.

Answers are on page 153.

3-21. *who/whom/whoever/whomever*

Who *and* whoever *are in the nominative (subjective) case and should be used only as subjects or predicate nominatives.* Whom *and* whomever *are in the objective case and should be used only as direct or indirect objects or as objects of a preposition.*

The following trick★ *can help you decide which word to use. First isolate the* who/whom *clause. Example:* Robert is the one (who/whom) we hope will become our new supervisor. *The isolated clause is* (who/whom) we hope will become our new supervisor. *Then delete* who/whom *from the sentence; there will be a gap in thought. Insert* he/she *or* him/her *in the gap (you may have to invert the word order):* We hope he will become our new supervisor. *If* he/she *makes sense, substitute* who; *if* him/her *is correct, substitute* whom. Robert is the one who we hope will become our new supervisor. *Change questions into statements before using this trick.*

Choose the correct word to complete each sentence.

1. Sam is the one (who/whom) will be hired.

2. Sam is the one (who/whom) the employer will hire.

3. The candidate (who/whom) smiles the most will be elected.

4. (Whoever/Whomever) submits the best proposal will be assigned to head the project.

5. (Whoever/Whomever) we elect as president should have a commitment to the council.

6. (Who/Whom) may I say is calling?

7. Give this letter to (whoever/whomever) arrives first.

8. To (who/whom) shall I address this package?

9. Ms. Smith, (who/whom) I met once before, will answer our questions about health insurance.

10. The question of (who/whom) should write the amendment was not decided.

11. The question of (who/whom) we should ask to write the amendment was not decided.

12. The committee wants to know (who/whom) you think should be in charge of the fund-raising campaign.

13. Cynthia is the one (who/whom) will renegotiate the contract.

14. (Who/Whom) did you talk to today about the computer repair?

15. (Whoever/Whomever) you appoint will do an excellent job.

Answers are on page 154.

---

*This trick is derived from *Questions You Always Wanted to Ask about English but Were Afraid to Raise Your Hand*, by Maxwell Nurnberg (New York: Pocket Books, 1972).

individual/person

The use of the word *individual* as a noun isn't wrong, but its use should be reserved for contrasting one human being with an organization or body of people: "How can an individual change the Communist regime in China?" or "Individuals and organizations have different needs." However, *individual* isn't synonymous with *person*, and substituting it for *person* lends a pretentious ring to a sentence. For example: "Any individuals who wish to take the CPR class should notify the personnel director" could be edited to read, "Anyone who wishes...."

3-22. Confusable Chestnuts

Use the correct form of the words in parentheses to complete the following sentences.

1. (lay, lie) I sometimes _____ the covers back, _____ abed, and _____ plans.

2. (loath, loathe) Marian is _____ to admit it, but she _____ gardening.

3. (aid, aide) The teacher's _____ came to the _____ of the injured child.

4. (palate, palette, pallet) Having just burned his _____ on hot coffee, the artist carefully set down his _____ and lay down to rest on his _____.

5. (cite, sight, site) The professor, who likes to _____ many sources, set his _____ on picking the best _____ for his research.

6. (principal, principle) The high school _____ operated according to his own _____.

7. (prophecy, prophesy) Elijah _____ to the people, but his _____ was ignored.

8. (lead, led) Yesterday the conductor _____ the choir from the podium; today he will _____ from the organ bench.

9. (foreword, forward) In the book's _____, the author invites the reader to look _____ into the next century.

10. (loose, lose) It's easy to _____ your perspective when chaotic forces are _____.

Answers on page 155.

3-23. Common Confusables

Here are some common confusables. See if you can explain the distinctions.

1. avenge/revenge
2. delegate/relegate
3. deplore/deprecate
4. nauseous/nauseated

5. notable/noticeable
6. persistence/perseverance
7. pervade/permeate
8. presume/assume

Answers are on page 156.

3-24. More Confusables

Choose the word in parentheses that will make each sentence correct.

1. During my interview with the vice president, I (implied, inferred) that she was looking for someone with more experience.

2. The author (implied, inferred) in the preface that the reclusive rock star had authorized the publication of this exclusive biography.

3. The best kind of mediator is one who is (disinterested, uninterested) in the outcome.

4. My guests were so (averse, adverse) to political discussion that I steered the conversation away from talk of the election.

5. The author was (enthused, enthusiastic) about the possibility that a producer might purchase film rights to his novel.

6. Because the climate in Arizona is so (healthful, healthy), the doctor suggested that her patient recuperate there.

7. Nudists (flaunt, flout) no laws when they (flaunt, flout) their physiques on Greek beaches.

Continued on next page

8. The (incredible, incredulous) prosecuting attorney pressed the defendant for more details about the day in question.

9. (Irregardless, regardless) of the outcome of the merger, all employees were guaranteed their jobs and their benefits.

10. For consumer protection, a fuel company in Florida now labels its products "flameable" instead of (flammable, inflammable).

Answers are on page 157.

3-1. Subject-Verb Agreement I

1. The pronoun *none* can be either singular or plural. In this sentence the singular is appropriate because there is only one scholarship to be won.

   What if **none** of our district's students **wins** the $5,000 scholarship?

2. A collective noun takes a singular verb if the group is working together as a unit. A collective noun requires a plural verb if the members of the group are working individually rather than as a group. If the plural verb bothers your ear, insert the words *the members of* before the collective noun.

   The **jury was** finally excused by the judge and left the courthouse.

   Or

   The **members** of the jury **were** finally excused by the judge and left the courthouse.

3. As the subject of a dependent clause, the pronoun *who*, *that*, or *which* can be either singular or plural, depending on the antecedent (the closest noun or pronoun to which it can refer). Because the antecedent of *who* is *contributors*, a plural noun, plural verbs are required. The sense of the sentence also indicates that there's more than one contributor.

   She is one of the few **contributors** who not only **donate** money but also **offer** time.

4. The pronoun *some*, like *none*, can be singular or plural. In this sentence the plural noun *sailboats* dictates a plural verb.

   Some of the **sailboats were** destroyed by the hurricane.

   When the noun is singular, the verb should be too: Some of the **pie was** eaten. Some of the **work was** unacceptable.

   Continued on next page

Explanation for sentences 5–7: These sentences contain quantitative expressions. When the subject of the sentence is the term *a percentage* or a fractional number such as *two-thirds*, the noun in the prepositional phrase that follows the subject, or is understood to follow it, determines the verb.

5. In this example, *correspondence* follows *of*, so the subject *two-thirds* requires a singular verb.

   Two-thirds of the correspondence **has** yet to be answered.

6. In this example, *freshmen* follows *of*, so the subject *two-thirds* requires a plural verb.

   Two-thirds of the freshmen **live** in dormitories.

7. In this example, *employees* follows *of*, so the subject *a small percentage* requires a plural verb.

   A small percentage of our employees **work** in this state but **live** in another state.

8. A sentence with a linking verb may have a singular subject and a plural complement or a plural subject and a singular complement. The verb should agree with the subject.

   The prime **concern is** better health care policies.

9. A singular verb is required when a phrase or clause functions as the subject of a sentence.

   Preparing income tax returns takes all my time during tax season.

10. Two singular subjects connected by the coordinate conjunction *and* require a plural verb. The subject of this sentence is two noun clauses.

    What our client wants to know and **what we want our client to know conflict** with what our attorney wants our client to know.

3-2. Subject-Verb Agreement II

1. When correlative conjunctions (*either…or, neither…nor, not only…but also*) or the coordinate conjunction *or* joins two subjects, the subject agrees with the verb closer to it. Since *proposals* is plural, the plural verb *are* is correct.

   Neither my new plan nor the committee's proposals are acceptable.

2. When a singular pronoun (*neither, either, anyone, each, someone,* and so on) functions as the subject, a singular verb is required. Since *neither* is singular, the verb *was* is correct.

   Neither of the proposals was acceptable.

3. Two subjects joined by *and* always require a plural verb.

   A designer and two graphic artists have been commissioned to work on the project.

4. A compound subject joined by anything other than *and* (*as well as, together with, in addition to,* or *along with*) requires a singular verb if the main subject is singular. If the sentence sounds awkward, recast it.

   A designer as well as two graphic artists has been commissioned to work on the project.

5. The subject of the dependent clause *who donate…and tend to wounded animals* is *who*, which can be either singular or plural. To determine the number of *who*, find the antecedent (the closest noun or pronoun to which it can refer); in this sentence, it is *veterinarians*, which is plural. Therefore, *who* requires the plural verbs *donate* and *tend*.

   Jessica Smith is one of the veterinarians who donate time to the local animal shelter and tend to wounded animals.

6. The subjects are the compound gerund phrases *being the oldest sibling in the family* and *knowing efficient ways of running a household*. Since compound subjects require a plural verb, the plural *have* is correct.

   Being the oldest sibling in the family and knowing efficient ways of running a household have not always worked to my advantage.

7. The subject of the main clause *one of…was on sale last week* is *one*, which is singular; therefore, the singular *was* is correct. The subject of

Continued on next page

the dependent clause *that create...and histograms* is the pronoun *that*, which can be singular or plural. To determine its number, find the antecedent; in this sentence, it's *programs*, which is plural. Therefore, the plural *create* is correct.

One of the software programs that create scatter plots and histograms was on sale last week.

8. The subject of the main clause *Rags...monthly service fee* is *Rags to Riches Investors*. Although the name is plural in form, it requires a singular verb because it represents a single organization. The pronoun *that* is the subject of the dependent clause *that claims...within a year* and refers to the singular noun *firm*; therefore, the singular *claims* is correct.

Rags to Riches Investors, a firm that claims to double clients' money within a year, charges a $50 monthly service fee.

9. The subjects of the sentence are the compound noun clauses *whether the jury believes the defendant* and *whether the judge allows certain evidence*. Compound subjects joined by *and* require plural verbs; therefore, the plural *remain* is correct.

Whether the jury believes the defendant and whether the judge allows certain evidence remain to be seen.

10. A collective noun can be either singular or plural. A collective is singular when the group is working together as a unit and plural when the members of the group are functioning individually. In this sentence, the members of the faculty are acting individually; therefore, plural verbs and a plural pronoun are correct.

When the faculty are not teaching, they are pursuing independent research projects.

11. The subject of the dependent clause *what appear to be pipe dreams* is *what*, which can be singular or plural. In this sentence, *what* refers to *dreams*, which is plural, so both *appear* and *are* are correct.

What appear to be pipe dreams are often profitable ideas.

12. The expression *the number of* requires a singular verb (the expression *a number of* requires a plural verb). The singular verb *seems* is correct.

The number of homeowners interested in planting trees seems to decrease every year.

3-3. Subject-Verb Agreement III

1. *directs, dances. Who* is the subject of the verbs in parentheses. The problem arises because *who* can be singular or plural, so you have to figure out which it is. Find the antecedent of *who* to determine its number. (The antecedent is the closest noun or pronoun to which the word can refer; *officer* is the antecedent here, and it's singular.)

   Nelson is the officer who directs traffic and dances at the same time.

2. *direct, dance.* The same rule holds true for this sentence; however, the antecedent of *who* is *officers*, a plural. It's true that a subject can't be in a prepositional phrase, and the word *officers* is the object of the preposition *of*. However, *officers* isn't the subject of the sentence; it's the antecedent of *who*. Here, the sentence deals with officers who direct traffic and dance at the same time. The first sentence dealt with one officer.

   Nelson is one of the officers who direct traffic and dance at the same time.

3. *directs, dances.* This sentence is an exception to the *who* rule. The words *the only one* restrict the meaning so that logically only a singular verb is possible: Only one officer directs and dances.

   Nelson is the only one of the officers who directs traffic and dances at the same time.

4. *are, smiles, says. Candidates* is the antecedent of *who* and is plural. Therefore, *are* is the correct answer. The subject of the other two verbs is *each*, which is singular and requires singular verbs.

   Each of the candidates who are running for office smiles too much and says too little.

5. *smiles, says.* The singular *candidate* is the subject and needs singular verbs. The intervening words *as well as* don't affect the subject, although commas would help convey this fact. If the sentence had read, "The candidate and her volunteers," plural verbs would be correct.

   The candidate as well as all her volunteers smiles too much and says too little.

Continued on next page

6. *believes, are.* In *neither…nor* constructions the verb agrees with the subject closer to it. Because the singular *doctor* is closer, the singular verb is correct. *All*, which is the subject of the second part of the sentence, can be either singular or plural. This sentence gives the sense of plurality, so the verb should be *are*. Let your ear help you in these situations.

    Neither the nurses nor the doctor believes in miracles, but all of them are hoping for one.

7. *believes, are.* The singular pronoun *neither* is the subject of the first part of the sentence; hence the singular verb *believes* is correct. In the second part of the sentence, the subject is the plural pronoun *both*; hence the plural verb is correct.

    Neither of the doctors believes in miracles, but, in these cases, both are hoping for one.

8. *is, are.* *Some* can be singular or plural. Because the first half of the sentence conveys a sense of singularity, *is* is correct. Because the second half of the sentence conveys the sense of plurality, *are* is correct. Again, let your ear help you.

    Since some of the manuscript is ready for the printer, some of the pages are to arrive by Friday.

9. *require* or *requires, want.* The word *data* is a plural form of *datum*, but it may be used with a plural or singular verb depending on whether the word refers primarily to facts or pieces of information (*these data require*) or to a body of information (*not much data is available*). *Media* is generally construed as plural and takes a plural verb.

    The data for the project requires immediate attention because the media want to disclose the findings.

    Or

    The data for the project require immediate attention because the media want to disclose the findings.

10. *am.* Because *I* is the antecedent of *who, am* is the correct verb, even though it sounds awkward.

    It is I, not they, who am responsible for conducting the survey.

3-4. Subject-Verb Agreement IV

1. *are, is.* The subject of the dependent clause is *that,* which has the plural *raises* as its antecedent (the closest noun or pronoun to which it can refer) and thus requires the plural verb. The subject of the main clause, which governs the verb in the second set of parentheses, is *decision,* which is singular and takes the singular *is.*

   Your decision about pay raises that **are** being deferred for six months **is** sure to win you no friends.

2. *was, live.* The word *half* can be singular or plural. In the dependent clause the sense of singularity (one mailing list) is implied, so *was* is the answer. In the independent clause the sense of plurality (people) is implied, so *live* is correct.

   When half of the mailing list **was** checked, we discovered that half of the people no longer **live** at the same address as five years ago.

3. *takes.* Because the subject is the singular gerund phrase *developing photographs, takes* is the correct verb.

   Developing photographs **takes** an enormous amount of time and patience.

4. *require.* The compound subject comprising two infinitive phrases takes the plural verb *require.*

   To copyedit and to proofread manuscripts **require** patience and skill.

5. *have, keeps. A number of* always takes a plural verb, and *the number of* always takes a singular verb. So the correct answers are *have* in the dependent clause and *keeps* in the independent clause.

   Although a number of managers **have** decided to avoid the confrontation, the number of assistant managers to accept the challenge **keeps** increasing.

6. *are.* The compound subject of *bookcase, desk,* and *computer* (the subjects come after the verb) requires the plural verb.

   There **are** a bookcase with broken shelves, a desk with no drawers, and a computer with no printer in my new office.

Continued on next page

7. *knows, equals, is, comes, results. Each* is singular, so *knows* is correct. When a subject expresses quantities that represent a total amount, the verb is singular.

   Each of the students **knows** that 3 plus 3 **equals** 6, that 16 minus 7 **is** 9, that 5 times 8 **comes** to 40, and that 81 divided by 9 **results** in 9.

8. *is.* Because the subject is the entire noun clause (*that…contracts*), the singular verb is correct.

   That they will accept the terms of the new contracts **is** almost definite.

9. *were, were, remain. Data* generally takes a plural verb; here *data* can certainly be construed as multiple pieces of information, so the plural is appropriate. *Criteria* is always plural and always takes a plural verb. (The singular is *criterion.*) Because the subject of the sentence is compound and joined by *and,* the verb must be the plural *remain.*

   Whether the data **were** correct and whether the criteria **were** accurate **remain** to be seen.

10. *elects, pass, cause.* The singular *public* is the subject of the first noun clause and takes a singular verb. *Voters,* the plural subject of the second noun clause, requires a plural verb. The two noun clauses joined by *and* are the subject of the sentence, so the plural *cause* is correct.

    Whom the public **elects** for the judiciary positions and which bond issues the voters **pass cause** the increase or decrease in taxes.

3-5.   Subject-Verb Agreement That 'Sounds' Wrong

1. Correct as written. *That* refers to *working groups* (pretty easy to spot, since it's preceded by *seven*) and so requires a plural verb.

   While heading one of the seven working groups that **make up** the association's task force on quality, Whitmore has earned a reputation for running efficient meetings.

2. Plural: *That* refers to *members* (not to *one* and, logically, not to *family*). Change the prepositional phrase to *in their mouths* to go with the plural construction.

The gaff-topsail catfish is one of several members of the catfish family that **carry** eggs in their mouths.

3. Correct as written. (This sentence is adapted from Edith Wharton's novel *The Custom of the Country*, New York: Knopf, 1994.)

He had never quite recovered from his attack of pneumonia, and the sudden rise in temperature—one of the fierce heat waves that **devastate** New York in the summer—was simply too much for him.

4. Plural: *That* refers to *programs*. Ask yourself: One of what? One of the programs. Which programs? Programs that entwine.

Although job training has usually been addressed on the local level, it is one of the emerging new programs that **entwine** community service and national concerns.

5. Plural: Again, one of what? The "freedoms that are included." (You could sidestep the problem by deleting *that are*. The sentence is then shorter and still makes sense.)

Voting is one of the most important freedoms that **are** included in the Constitution.

6. Singular: *That* refers to *the only one*. Logically, it must be singular. The remaining boats have one or the other; the *Beverly* is unique. (Watch for *only* as a clue in constructions of this type.) You could also delete *that is*.

The *Beverly* is the only one of the boats that **is** equipped with both a motor and a sail.

7. Plural: *That* refers to *images*—images "that come to me."

I'm not sure why, but a hovering hummingbird is one of the images that **come** to me as I puzzle out how to resolve my newest staffing problem.

8. Plural: *That* refers to *members*. One of what? Members. Which members? The members who have already paid.

If you are not one of the members who **have** already paid this year's dues, please use the coupon on the back page and send your payment today.

Continued on next page

9. Correct as written. As in number 6, *only* is the clue to the singular construction.

   At Sunday's graduation ceremonies, Lynne—who uses a wheelchair—will be the only one in her class who has never missed a day of school.

10. Plural: *That* refers to *approaches*.

    Known as program H-1B, it is one of the few approaches that allow foreign professionals to work legally in the United States while seeking permanent residence here.

11. Correct as written. Remember, with *or* and *nor*, the verb agrees with the subject closer to it, which in this sentence is the plural *more*.

    One or more of the rules that explain subject-verb agreement are often misinterpreted.

3-6. Will the Real Subject Please Stand Up?

1. Singular: *Who*, the subject of the modifying clause, refers to *office-holder*, so the verb is singular.

   She is the first office-holder in recent years who has been able to forge significant ties with both ethnic minorities and separatist leaders.

2. Correct as written: The subject of the dependent clause, *that*, refers to *study*.

   Relying almost wholly on a long-since-disproved theory, the author never mentions the intensive and well-documented scholarly study of the ruins that has taken place in the past 20 years.

3. Singular: The verb must agree with the subject (*alternative*), not the complement (*mailing lists*).

   An alternative to newsgroups is mailing lists.

   If you prefer the sound of a plural verb, rewrite the sentence:

   Newsgroups are an alternative to mailing lists.

4. Plural: The three-part subject joined by *and* requires a plural verb.

   His demonstrated **leadership**, deep community **roots, and** progressive **stand** on local issues **make** him an attractive candidate for the County Board.

   If the sentence, although correct, sounds wrong to you, rewrite it so that the plural noun right beside the verb doesn't seem to govern:

   The **combination** of his demonstrated leadership, deep community roots, and progressive stand on local issues **makes** him an attractive candidate for the County Board.

5. Correct as written—at least if we assume that the three together constitute the headliners, thereby making them a *trio*, which is itself a singular subject. (Isn't English wonderful?)

   A **trio** of top bluegrass bands **headlines** the annual spring concert.

6. Singular: The subject is *training*. Don't be sidetracked by the prepositional phrase.

   The professor outlined three reasons why **training** in speaking, reading, and acting **is** helpful in vocal improvement.

7. Plural: *Routers*, the antecedent of *that*, is plural.

   E-mail messages pass through a **series** of routers that **direct** them to their intended destinations.

8. Singular: Be consistent in all references to the organization; such names are usually best treated as singular. Note *has* in the main clause, and change *their* to *its*.

   The **Women's Philharmonic**, which made **its** East Coast debut in a recent performance, **has** a revolutionary goal—to change what is played in every concert hall by incorporating the work of women composers into the orchestral repertoire.

9. Plural: The two-part subject is joined by *and*.

   We propose a workshop approach for this project because the **variation** in individual goals **and** the **need** for group interaction **require** integrated planning and evaluation.

Continued on next page

10. This one's tricky. We can't leave *Disney* singular in the first clause of the indirect quote and plural in the second; the simplest solution is to delete *they* and make the verb singular.

    If you asked me about the film version of the Pocahontas story, I'd say that **Disney** does entertainment and **does** it very well.

11. Use a plural verb in the first clause to go with the two-part subject and a singular verb in the second clause to go with *inclusiveness*.

    He argued that widespread **prejudice and discrimination** still **exist**, although greater **inclusiveness** in education and hiring **has** greatly benefited society as a whole.

12. Correct as written: The compound subject is joined by *and*.

    The **Pentagon and** the **Base Closing Commission have** criteria that apply to each base.

3-7. The Subjunctive: Wishful Thinking?

1. Incorrect: Sentences that express suggestions, demands, or requirements take the subjunctive, not the indicative. The third-person-singular *mother* needs the present subjunctive form *remember*. If the subjunctive sounds awkward, recast the sentence in the indicative.

   It's important that your mother **remember** to anchor the boat.

   Or

   Your mother must **remember** to anchor the boat.

2. It depends on the meaning: Whether the *were* is correct depends on how likely it is that Weber will be the lifeguard. Sentences that are improbable or contrary to fact take the subjunctive. If Weber is a tourist visiting Maui, complaining about a lazy lifeguard, the subjunctive is correct.

   "If I **were** the lifeguard, I would never fall asleep...."

   But if Weber is interviewing for a lifeguard job that he's likely to get, the indicative is correct.

   "If I **was** the lifeguard, I would never fall asleep...."

As *The New York Public Library Writer's Guide to Style and Usage* puts it, improbable, doubtful, or contrary-to-fact statements take the subjunctive "in the past tense to express present time." But "*if, as if,* or *as though* do not always signal the subjunctive mood. The indicative tells the reader that the information in the dependent clause could possibly be true."

3. Correct: *Be that as it may* is a standard phrase that uses the subjunctive. Others are *far be it from me, so be it, come what may, if I were you, suffice it to say,* and *as it were.*

   "Jamal likes to wear black shoes. Be that as it may," Sandra said, "he needs to wear brown shoes with a brown suit."

4. Correct: The last sentence makes it clear that the speaker is unlikely to own a ranch. The *if* clause, therefore, takes the subjunctive. Just apply the rule on sentences that are improbable, doubtful, or contrary to fact.

   If I were living on a 70-acre ranch, I would own 3 dogs, 12 chickens, and as many horses as the land would hold. But unless I find a bag of cash in the basement, I'll be living in this tiny house forever.

5. Incorrect: Like sentence 1, this sentence falls into the suggestion, demand, or requirement category and needs the subjunctive unless reworded to avoid it.

   The rabbi asked that the congregation sit.

   Or

   The rabbi asked the congregation to sit.

6. Incorrect: *Words Into Type* uses this as an example where a subjunctive should not be used. Was the ground clear? The speaker is trying to figure out which equally probable condition exists.

   Next I looked to see if the ground was clear.

7. Incorrect: The sister isn't and probably will never be her sibling's boss, so use the subjunctive.

   If I were your boss instead of your sister, I'd fire you.

8. Correct: The son isn't actually present, so the wish expresses a condition that's contrary to fact.

   Anse wished bitterly that his son were there to see the new tractor.

Continued on next page

9. Correct: The dependent clause expresses a requirement, so it takes the subjunctive *be sent* (follows the same rule as sentences 1 and 5).

Our handbook requires that acceptance letters **be sent** out within a week of application.

10. Incorrect: Because the *if* statement is in the present conditional tense, the consequence is in the simple future tense. If the first verb were past tense, the consequence would be present conditional.

If stocks **fall,** much of executive pay **will evaporate**.

Or

If stocks **fell,** much of executive pay **would evaporate**.

3-8. Verb Forms

Present	Past	Past Participle
bear	bore	borne
beat	beat	beat or beaten
burst[1]	burst	burst
creep	crept	crept
dive[2]	dived or dove	dived or dove
drink	drank	drunk
get	got	got or gotten
hang[3]	hanged or hung	hanged or hung
lay	laid	laid
lead	led	led
lend	lent	lent
lie	lay	lain
prove[4]	proved or proven	proved or proven
raise	raised	raised
rise	rose	risen
shine	shone or shined	shone or shined

sing	sang	sung
sink	sank	sunk
smell	smelled or smelt	smelled or smelt
sneak[5]	sneaked	sneaked
spring	sprang	sprung
swim	swam	swum
wake[2]	waked or woke	waked or woken

---

[1]Don't confuse the verb *burst* with the verb *bust*. *Bust* is slang and therefore unacceptable in formal writing—despite a recent newspaper head blaring that "Spring Is Busting Out."

[2]According to *The American Heritage Dictionary of the English Language*, 3rd edition (*AHD*), "Regional American dialects vary in the way that certain verbs form their principal parts. Northern dialects seem to favor forms that change the internal vowel in the verb—hence *dove* for the past tense of *dive*, and *woke* for *wake*: *They woke up with a start*. Southern dialects, on the other hand, tend to prefer forms that add an *-ed* to form the past tense and the past participle of these same verbs: *The children dived into the swimming hole. The baby waked up early*."

[3]People are *hanged*; pictures are *hung*.

[4]According to *AHD*, "*Proved* is actually the older form of the past participle; *proven* is a Scottish variant that was first introduced into wider usage in legal contexts: *The jury ruled that the charges were not proven*. Both forms are now well established in written English as participles: *He has proved (or proven) his point. The claims have not been proved (or proven)*. However, *proven* is more common when the word is used as an adjective before a noun: *a proven talent*."

[5]*AHD* lists *snuck* as a variant and says it is now widely used by educated speakers and respected writers. In formal written English, however, "*snuck* still meets with much resistance" because of its nonstandard origins, and 67 percent of the *AHD* Usage Panel disapproves of it.

3-9.   Feeling Tense and Moody

Relatively few reference books address the use of the conditional in any detail. *Words Into Type* offers counsel:

> Always consider the tense of a dependent verb form in relation to the time expressed in the verb upon which it depends.

> Wrong: How would natural conditions be affected if water continued to contract until it freezes?

> Right:…until it froze?

Continued on next page

Would be affected, the governing main verb, is in the past subjunctive tense; in the dependent clause that begins with *if*, *water continued to contract* correctly uses past tense—so, too, *froze* should follow. This example takes care of three of the problem sentences:

2. All Americans would suffer in some way if benefits for Social Security or Medicare **fell**.

4. The accounts rely on the theory that existing capital would suffer a drop in value when an investment incentive **rose**, in the same way that a bond would if the interest rate **rose**.

6. Even if such consumers could repay a loan out of their prospective earnings, lenders **might** not extend one because it could not be secured by a real asset.

Words Into Type goes on to say,

Sometimes the subordinate verb fixes the time and the principal verb requires correction....

Wrong: If the unexpired subscriptions had amounted to $80,000, instead of $20,000, the adjusting entry would take the following form.

Right: ...would have taken the following form.

In sentence 3, the principal verb could be made subjunctive to match the subordinate verbs:

3. If discretionary spending **were** frozen, the deficit would rise in 1997 and 1998 but would then begin to decline.

An alternative would be to leave *is* in the indicative mood and change the subordinate verbs:

3. If discretionary spending is frozen, the deficit **will** rise in 1997 and 1998 but **will** then begin to decline.

The choice depends on the context. The author may consider a freeze in spending unlikely, in which case the principal verb should be in the subjunctive. If the author is presenting the spending freeze as one of several alternatives, all equally likely, the indicative/future version of the sentence is a better choice. By that logic, sentence 2 could be written like this:

2. All Americans **will** suffer in some way if benefits for Social Security or Medicare **fall**.

It's relatively simple to match the sequence of tenses when you're sure what the mood of the sentence should be. A thornier problem is deciding whether to use the subjunctive. *The Handbook of Good English*, by Edward D. Johnson (New York: Pocket Books, 1991), has a useful discussion of this point:

> Clauses that begin with *if* or *as if* are not always subjunctive. *If he is rich he will be welcome* is indicative; the *if* clause presents a condition that may be true. *He acts as if his life is in danger* and *He acts as if his life were in danger* are both correct; the indicative *as if* clause in the first sentence implies that his life may well be in danger, and the subjunctive *as if* clause in the second sentence implies that it is unlikely that his life is in danger....

Johnson's *Handbook* also zeros in on the very situation that our correspondent confronts. As an example, it quotes a sentence from a 1981 speech by President Reagan: "If there were some kind of international crisis, we would correct that with new legislation." Johnson notes that Reagan was

> ...using the...subjunctive for a conditional sentence about the future, which cannot logically be a condition contrary to fact. This use of the subjunctive is one of those that grammarians have been waving farewell to for decades, but it has remained alive and seems to be becoming more common....

> Use of the distinctive *were* forms for the future conditional is defensible; it permits expression of a special degree of doubt about the future condition. It has always been common among the well-educated. It is perhaps a bit fussy, but it does not invite derision the way *It is I* and *Whom do you want to invite?* may.

Sentences 1 and 5 can be tweaked to make both clauses conditional:

1. **The rules would require that the Congress adjust tax schedules so that overall growth in real incomes would not push people into higher income tax brackets.**

5. **The size of the future problem is so great that eliminating the deficit by 2002 would not alone ensure that future deficits remained at an acceptable level without additional changes in spending and taxes.**

3-10. The Placement of Modifiers

The correct placement of modifiers to avoid ambiguity or illogical statements depends on the meaning. In some cases, only the writer can know; an editor should ask rather than make inferences.

1. Misplaced modifier: **The thieves were apprehended by the police soon after the convenience store was robbed.**

2. Dangling modifier: **While we were cooking for twelve people, the power went off because of the electrical storm.**

3. Dangling modifier: **Rushing to meet the Friday deadline, the editors were unable to give the manuscript a final polishing.**

4. Squinting modifier: **When the seminar was over, the instructor told the participants they would receive certificates.**

   Or (depending on meaning)

   The instructor told the participants that they would receive certificates when the seminar was over.

5. Dangling modifier: **To understand the proposal for the new training program completely, senior managers should review all the supervisors' recommendations.**

6. Misplaced modifier: **While running through the park, the jogger saw the sailboats racing.**

7. Squinting modifier: **People who occasionally exercise may have some minor aches and pains.**

   Or (depending on meaning)

   People who exercise may occasionally have some minor aches and pains.

8. Dangling modifier: **After the upgraded telephone system is installed, every telephone line can be answered from anywhere in the office.**

9. Misplaced modifier: **To keep teeth healthy, everyone should have a dental checkup at least twice a year.**

3-11.   Misplaced Modifiers

1.   The limiting modifier *only* is misplaced. The sentence really means that except for one day a week my son was unprepared.

   The teacher said that my son did his homework only on Wednesdays.

2.   The word *eventually* is squinting. Does it modify *told* or *purchase?* Depending on the meaning, there are three possible correct positions for *eventually* in this sentence.

   The coordinator of the adult education program eventually told us the institution would purchase new computers for the lab.

   Or

   Eventually the coordinator of the adult education program told us the institution would purchase new computers for the lab.

   Or

   The coordinator of the adult education program told us the institution would eventually purchase new computers for the lab.

3.   An introductory verbal phrase is understood to modify the nearest noun or pronoun. This sentence says the woodpecker was looking through the field glasses (the true subject has been left out).

   While adjusting his new field glasses, he saw a red-headed woodpecker land on a nearby branch.

4.   As this sentence stands, the discrepancy recalculated the totals. Changing the introductory phrase to a clause is one solution.

   When I recalculated the tax return totals, the discrepancy between my accountant's results and the IRS's results became apparent.

5.   This sentence says that a four-year-old was the director of marketing.

   When Kate was four years old, her father was transferred to San Francisco to direct the marketing division.

6.   This sentence implies that the youngster should start mowing the previous evening—a physical impossibility. What the writer probably meant was that the suggestion was made last night.

   Last night he suggested that our 12-year-old start mowing the lawn.

Continued on next page

7. The customer must have been a bit chilly. The flowers, of course, were in the refrigerated showcase.

Madeline showed the customer the available flowers in the refrigerated showcase.

8. The question is, Who has the money? In one case, commas will solve the problem. In the other, the phrase should be moved.

While the bank teller stood still, grasping the money tightly, the robber darted forward.

Or

While the bank teller stood still, the robber darted forward grasping the money tightly.

3-12. Shifty Adverbs

1. **Foolishly** hoping for good seats at the movie theater, we were tempted to drive faster.

   Or

   Hoping for good seats at the movie theater, we were **foolishly** tempted to drive faster.

   This test sentence can be read both ways. In the first answer, *foolishly hoping* sounds more natural than *hoping foolishly*, and in the second, no one would say *tempted foolishly*.

2. We were glad to have **finally** pinpointed the problem.

   Not splitting the infinitive here would be awkward.

3. Will this software help us to **better** achieve the graphic effects we want?

   To achieve better would be awkward in this sentence as well.

4. Our friend the acquisitions editor told us that he had **at last** found the manuscript that would make his career: *Collecting Cuban Cigars.*

   At last modifies *found*, so that's where it should be placed.

5. I'm telling the truth—I could **never** in a million years have made up something like that.

    It might be better to say, *I couldn't have made up something like that....*

6. The art director can look at a page and **spontaneously** think of better ways it could have been designed.

    Spontaneously modifies *think*; it sounds better if it precedes the verb.

7. Many editors type up a page-by-page query cover sheet that **more fully** explains the marginal notes.

    More fully modifies *explains* and again sounds better if it precedes the verb.

8. **Unfortunately,** this seems to be our only option.

    In this case, *unfortunately* modifies the sentence as a whole, not any particular word. Such "editorial" comments are usually placed at the beginning of a sentence.

9. If you plan to **completely** renovate the bathroom, you'll need a permit.

    Completely could follow *bathroom*, and some people would say it that way, but if you replace *completely* with *partially*, most speakers would place it between *to* and *renovate*.

10. *Only* is a limiting modifier. By varying its placement, you can give this sentence six different meanings:

    1. **Only** he said that he loved me. (No one else said it.)

    2. He **only** said that he loved me. (He didn't mean it.)

    3. He said **only** that he loved me. (That's all he said.)

    4. He said that **only** he loved me. (No one else loved me.)

    5. He said that he **only** loved me. (He didn't like me, and he didn't respect me.)

    6. He said that he loved **only** me. (He didn't love anyone else.)

        Or

        He said that he loved me **only**. (He didn't love anyone else.)

3-13.   Adverb or Adjective? Confusion with -*ly* Words

1. If the adverb *badly* were used in this sentence to modify the verb *feels*, the sentence would mean that she has nerve damage on the ends of her fingers. What's actually happening is that the adjective *bad* is modifying the pronoun *she*. *Feel* is functioning in this sentence as a linking verb, and it makes sense if you substitute *is*—*She is bad*.

   She feels **bad**.

2. In this sentence the adverb *badly* is needed because it modifies the verb *was hurt*.

   He was not hurt very **badly** when he collided with another skater on the ice.

3. In this sentence the adjective *loud* is modifying the noun *bell*. (It also makes sense to say *The bell is loud*.)

   The bell sounded **loud**.

4. Either the adjective or adverb may be correct, depending on the context of the sentence. If *quiet* is modifying *he*, then the adjective is correct. However, if stage directions are involved, for example, the actor could be waiting behind the curtains and then he could appear quietly on the stage.

   He appeared **quiet**. (*quiet* modifies *he*)

   He appeared **quietly**. (*quietly* modifies *appeared*)

5. Try substituting *was* in this sentence—*He was (careful, carefully) along the runner of the bobsled for any flaws*. The sentence doesn't make sense, so the adverb is correct because it modifies the action verb *felt*.

   He felt **carefully** along the runner of the bobsled for any flaws.

3-14.   Pin Down Vague Terms of Measurement

Each vague term is followed by the unanswered questions that readers are
left wondering about.

1. **virtually all.** What percentage of the women present went to the
   Mac workshop? It's hard to decide where the emphasis belongs: on the
   preference of women as opposed to that of men for the design seminar
   or on the preference of women for design as opposed to spreadsheet
   training. If men were present, what percentage of all participants went
   to the Mac seminar?

2. **as soon as possible.** When should the letter be answered? By the
   close of business or by the end of the week?

3. **in bulk/substantial discount.** What cutoff point defines a bulk
   purchase? What's the retail price and how much will it be discounted?
   What's the savings?

4. **a time or two/lately.** How many times has it actually happened in
   the past week? In the past six months? How many other people are
   regularly asked to stay late? (Also note that *only* is misplaced.)

5. **high winds/terrible destruction/small community.** What
   was the force of the wind in miles per hour? What was the estimated
   property damage? What are the population and the size of the area
   affected? If millions of dollars in repairs are needed for a few square
   miles, the magnitude of the damage is clear.

6. **slight majority.** What was the margin? What percentage of the
   eligible voters did the majority vote represent? This victory could
   still have been significant if the narrow margin represented a large
   popular vote.

7. **a short while/more than a few.** How many years have you
   worked for the paper? Does that include the time you were a gofer or
   just the time you've been a reporter? How long does it usually take to
   develop contacts? How many of them do you have? Three? Twelve?
   The way this sentence is worded, it's a slightly invidious compliment.

8. **breakneck speed.** How fast were they driving? What was the speed
   limit? Are they teenagers who go 70 miles an hour without realizing it
   or retirees pulling a trailer who feel reckless at 45 miles an hour?

Continued on next page

9. **minimal amount of effort.** How many hours will the staff have to work? Will everyone have to work or will only a few people devote time to the project?

3-15.   Precision in the Choice of Words

1. *Further* means "to a greater degree or extent." *Farther*, which is the precise word choice here, refers to actual, measurable distance.

   Because Dale lives **farther** from the convention center than I do, I will attend the conference.

2. *Less* refers to quantity or degree and is used with singular nouns. *Fewer*, the correct choice, refers to countable items and is used with plural nouns.

   After our company contracted with a new printer, our proofreader found **fewer** mistakes than usual.

3. Both *anxious* and *eager* mean "desirous," but *anxious* implies fear or concern and is a negative term; *eager* is a positive term.

   Since I was **eager** to buy a new car, I was thrilled with both my promotion and my raise.

4. Use *between* when referring to two persons or things and *among* when referring to more than two persons or things.

   The bonus money was divided evenly **among** the training, graphics, editing, and proofreading departments.

5. Use *disappointed in* when referring to a person, plan, hope, or result. Use *disappointed with* when referring to a thing.

   The client was **disappointed in** the printer because the newsletters were delivered late.

6. When used as a singular compound pronoun, *everyone* is treated as one word. *Every one* and *any one* are two words when they're followed by an *of* phrase or when used to mean "one of a number of things."

   By next spring, **every one** of the employees will be eligible to participate in the new training program.

7. *Insure* means "to protect against loss." *Ensure* means "to make certain." *Assure* means "to give someone confidence."

    To **ensure** that our budget proposal is correct, our supervisor asked us to triple-check our figures.

8. *Due to* introduces an adjective phrase and should modify nouns; it's normally used after some form of the verb *to be* (*is, are, was, were*, etc.): The change in plans was due to the unexpected arrival of the president of the university. The precise word choice here is *because of.* When used correctly, *because of* and *on account of* introduce adverbial phrases that modify verbs.

    Because of his poor health, Mr. Saltz decided to resign from his stressful job.

9. In everyday usage, the word *percent* should always be preceded by a number; for example, *30 percent, 0.2 percent, 120 percent.* Similarly, a column of figures in a table may be headed *Percent of Total, Percent of Return*, etc. (In American usage, *percent* is preferred to *per cent*; use of the percent sign should be avoided in formal text.) In all other situations, use the term *percentage.*

    A large **percentage** of registered voters went to the polls in inclement weather to support their candidates.

10. The verb *lay* means "to put or place." Its principal parts are *lay, laid, laid*, and *laying.* The principal parts of the verb *lie*, which means "to recline, rest, or stay" or "to take a position of rest," are *lie, lay, lain*, and *lying.* In the sentence, the manuscript has stayed on the desk for three days, so the verb *lain* is correct.

    This report has **lain** untouched on my desk for three days.

3-16. More on Precise Words

1. *Comprise* means "to include, contain, consist of"; *compose* means "to make up." The parts *compose* (make up) the whole; the whole *comprises* (includes) the parts or the whole is *composed of* (not *is comprised of*) the parts.

    The new corporation **comprises** (or *is composed of*) five major divisions.

    Continued on next page

2. *Like* is a preposition. Although *like* is widely used as a conjunction in colloquial speech, use *as* or *as if* in written material.

   Although we have encountered many problems, it looks as if we will meet the manager's unreasonable deadline.

3. Use *from* after the verb *graduated*. The verb forms *graduated from* and *was graduated from* are both acceptable (although the former has virtually replaced the latter).

   After six long, grueling years, my son finally graduated from Boston University.

4. *Infer* means "to assume, to deduce, to arrive at a conclusion." You infer something from another person's words or actions. *Imply* means "to suggest." You imply something by your own words or actions.

   The supervisor implied in his pep talk that the publications department would receive a substantial bonus if the proposal was a success.

5. *Unique* means "being the only one." Don't use *unique* to mean "unusual." *Unique* is an absolute and can't be modified by *more, most, very, somewhat, rather,* or *comparatively*. However, it can be modified by *quite, almost, nearly, really, surely, perhaps, absolutely,* or *in some respects*.

   Of all the presentations about new software products, the ABC Company's was unique.

6. Use the preposition *in* with *disappointed* when referring to a person, plan, hope, or result. Use the preposition *with* when referring to a thing.

   The word processing operators were disappointed with the new spell-check software because it did not highlight repeated words.

7. Use the preposition *of* with *enamored* when referring to a person. Use the preposition *with* when referring to an object: *enamored with the new football stadium*.

   Rebecca, an inexperienced secretary, was so enamored of her boss that she thought he could do no wrong.

8. The verb *allude* means "to refer indirectly"; *elude* means "to dodge or slip away from"; *illude* (a rarely used word) means "to cheat, mock, play tricks upon (in the manner of a magician)."

The clever hotel magnate managed to **elude** IRS scrutiny by falsifying his income tax forms.

9. *Compliment* means "to make a flattering remark"; *complement* means "to make complete."

The illustrator's ability to draw **complemented** the author's ability to tell a story.

10. The words *adversary*, *enemy*, and *foe* imply hostile opposition. A *foe* is more actively hostile than an *enemy*, and an *enemy* is more actively hostile than an *adversary*. (An *antagonist* or *opponent* may be in opposition to someone else, but the *antagonist* or *opponent* may not be hostile at all.)

Although the law partners were **opponents** on the tennis court, they always agreed on legal issues.

3-17. Using the Right Idiomatic Prepositions

1. The inexperienced teacher was **annoyed by** the poor conduct of the students.

Be annoyed by something; *feel annoyed with* someone.

2. Although Morton was **angry with** himself for overlooking such a blatant error, he decided to make the best of a bad situation.

Angry at an action; *angry with* a person.

3. I **concur in** the opinion that this company needs a reorganization of managerial responsibilities.

Concur in a common decision or proposition; *concur with* other persons in their views.

4. As an **advocate of** free speech, she supported the court's decision.

Used as a noun, *advocate* takes *of*; used as a verb, *advocate* takes *for*.

Continued on next page

5. When she **parted from** her colleagues to take a new job, she was not sure whether she would ever see them again.

   Part from a person; *part with* a possession.

6. The students were so **preoccupied with** evaluating the results of the experiment that they didn't notice they were the only two left in the lab.

   Preoccupied by—engaged with—a person; *preoccupied with* a thing or an activity.

7. His **affinity with** open spaces forced him out of the megalopolis and into rural America.

   Bernstein says that if you think of affinity as meaning "a tie of kinship, sympathy, or attraction, you will use *between*, *with*, or sometimes *to*, and you will discard *for*. And you will be right."

8. Today's emphasis on plain English seems **analogous to** Franklin Roosevelt's belief that plain words reach more people.

   The only correct preposition is *to*.

9. **Compared with** last year's losses, this year's balance sheet looks promising.

   Compare to is used for making a metaphoric or general comparison; *compare with* is used for indicating similarities or differences of size or other specifics. According to Bernstein, "The choice…is not a matter of indifference.…Since *compare to* is more often involved in figurative constructions, whereas *compare with* is the more literal, everyday phrase, the uses calling for *with* far outnumber those calling for *to*."

3-18. More Right Prepositions

1. Because George was **careless in** his editing, he lost his job.

   Careless about dress, *in* one's work, *of* the feelings of others.

2. The manager was so **disgusted by** her supervisor's swearing that she asked for a transfer to another department.

   Disgusted at an action, *by* a quality or habit of a person or animal, *with* a person.

3. The antique furniture presented a **contrast to** the high-tech architecture of the office building.

Contrast between this and that, this *presents a contrast to* that, this is *in contrast with* that.

4. **Ranging from** 230 **to** 250 degrees, the oil bath was preferred to the water bath for the experiment.

Ranging between boundaries, *from* x *to* y degrees, *within* a territory.

5. Mr. Jacobs was unable to hide his **resentment against** his supervisor, Ms. Simmons, when she rejected his reorganization plan.

Resentment against a person, *at* (or *for*) a wrong.

6. A substantive editor must be **attentive to** tone and readability, as well as **to** organization and content.

The only correct preposition is *to*.

7. Being **well educated in** the field of civil engineering, Ms. Hogan was an excellent candidate for the position of department manager.

Educated about (or *concerning*) the needs of life, *for* living, *in* a field of study. The sentence is correct as is.

8. A believer in saving the environment, David was willing to **labor for** the recycling movement in his community.

Labor at a task, *for* (or *in*) a cause, *under* a taskmaster, *with* tools.

9. The writer was **wary of** the inexperienced editor's being responsible for reorganizing the manuscript.

The only correct preposition is *of*.

3-19. Second Cousin Exercise

1. The correct spelling is *nitpicker*. *Knitpicker* isn't a word.

He was the worst **nitpicker** I've ever seen.

Continued on next page

2. Although the term *podium* can be used to mean a lectern, its primary meaning is the platform an orchestral conductor stands on.

The speaker placed her notes on the lectern.

3. *Hone* means to sharpen. *Home in* comes from the early days of aviation when pilots navigated by tuning their receivers to radio beacons and then homing in on them.

We should try to home in on what the real problem is.

4. *Emend* is now reserved for making editorial changes in documents. *Amend*—to change or improve—is what legislators do to laws.

The editor carefully emended the text.

5. A *boycott* is a refusal to buy, sell, or use, while an *embargo* is an order from a government prohibiting the departure of commercial ships from its ports.

To prevent the enemy from importing missiles, the President ordered an embargo (or *a blockade*) of the harbor.

6. You can *pour* water; a book is *pored over*.

He pored over the dusty manuscript for hours.

7. *Importantly* connotes doing something "in an important manner." *Important* is correct here. *Stemmed from*, rather than *centered around*, is the preferred choice here.

More important, the whole problem stemmed from a misunderstanding.

8. *Convince* shouldn't be followed by an infinitive.

Joe tried to persuade me to buy a 40-volume encyclopedia.

9. To take note of an existing condition is to *cite* it. The examples cited were *discrete*, or separate, not modest.

In his report, the engineer cited several discrete examples of poor design practice.

3-20. *that* vs. *which* and *who*

1. Restrictive. *Which is* should either be changed to *that is* or deleted.

   The team responsible for drafting the Strategic Alignment Policy Summary reports directly to the president.

2. The first clause can be read as restrictive or nonrestrictive, and the second is nonrestrictive.

   The SAPS team **that** has been working overtime on the policy manual, **which** is overdue, sent out for pizza.

3. Both are nonrestrictive. The adverb carries more force if it's moved to the end of the sentence, though it can be left before *declining*.

   "Strategic alignment," a plan for a 50 percent reduction in force, is key to doubling corporate income, **which** has been declining steadily.

4. Definitely restrictive.

   Corporate communicators often can't combat the rumors **that** circulate in the wake of management transitions.

5. All restrictive. The relative pronoun doesn't need repeating in the first clause, and the pronoun in the second should be changed from *that* to *who* because the antecedent is *employees* (persons, not inanimate objects).

   Positions **that** are not key and are left open because of disgruntled employees **who** retire early will not be filled.

6. Restrictive, nonrestrictive.

   Documents published by the Office of Technology Assessment, **which** has been abolished, are still available through the Superintendent of Documents, P.O. Box 371954, Pittsburgh, PA 15250-7974.

7. Nonrestrictive, restrictive.

   Portable Document Format (PDF), **which** is an almost exact replica of the printed product, is one way documents can be made available on the Internet.

Continued on next page

8. Restrictive.

   The Institute for Federal Printing and Publishing is offering a service to its customers **who** elect to receive reminders of upcoming classes by fax.

9. Restrictive, nonrestrictive, restrictive.

   A thorough procedure guide prepared by Conference Call USA, **which** is a provider of teleconferencing services, explained to participants **who** wanted to retrieve printed materials how to use fax-on-demand.

10. Restrictive, nonrestrictive.

    Memories of people, places, and things **that** meant a lot to my parents were carefully preserved in scrapbooks, **which** we showed to the children on our last visit.

11. The first clause can be either restrictive or nonrestrictive. The second is definitely restrictive.

    Downsizing the workforce, **which** grew in the 1980s, is a task no company undertakes gladly.

3-21. *who/whom/whoever/whomever*

1. Sam is the one **who** will be hired. (**He** will be hired.)

2. Sam is the one **whom** the employer will hire. (The employer will hire **him**.)

3. The candidate **who** smiles the most will be elected. (**He/She** smiles the most.)

4. **Whoever** submits the best proposal will be assigned to head the project. (**He/She** submits the best proposal.)

5. **Whomever** we elect as president should have a commitment to the council. (We elect **him/her**. The entire clause *whomever we elect* is the subject of the verb phrase *should have*.)

6. **Who** may I say is calling? (I may say **he/she** is calling.)

7. Give this letter to **whoever** arrives first. (**He/She** arrives first.)

8. To **whom** shall I address this package? (I shall address this package to **him/her**.)

9. Ms. Smith, **whom** I met once before, will answer our questions about health insurance. (I met **her** once before.)

10. The question of **who** should write the amendment was not decided. (**He/She** should write the amendment.)

11. The question of **whom** we should ask to write the amendment was not decided. (We should ask **him/her** to write the amendment.)

12. The committee wants to know **who** you think should be in charge of the fund-raising campaign. (You think **he/she** should be in charge.)

13. Cynthia is the one **who** will renegotiate the contract. (**She** will renegotiate the contract.)

14. **Whom** did you talk to today about the computer repair? (You talked to **him/her** today.)

15. **Whomever** you appoint will do an excellent job. (You appoint **him/her**. The entire clause *whomever you appoint* is the subject of the verb phrase *will do*.)

3-22. Confusable Chestnuts

1. *lay/lie/lay.* I sometimes **lay** the covers back, **lie** abed, and **lay** plans.

2. *loath/loathes.* Marian is **loath** to admit it, but she **loathes** gardening.

3. *aide/aid.* The teacher's **aide** came to the **aid** of the injured child.

Continued on next page

4. *palate/palette/pallet.* Having just burned his **palate** on hot coffee, the artist carefully set down his **palette** and lay down to rest on his **pallet**.

5. *cite/sights/site.* The professor, who likes to **cite** many sources, set his **sights** on picking the best **site** for his research.

6. *principal/principles.* The high school **principal** operated according to his own **principles**.

7. *prophesied/prophecy.* Elijah **prophesied** to the people, but his **prophecy** was ignored.

8. *led/lead.* Yesterday the conductor **led** the choir from the podium; today he will **lead** from the organ bench.

9. *foreword/forward.* In the book's **foreword**, the author invites the reader to look **forward** into the next century.

10. *lose/loose.* It's easy to **lose** your perspective when chaotic forces are **loose**.

3-23.   Common Confusables

1. *avenge/revenge:* These words were once interchangeable, but today *avenge* suggests legitimate vindication (an avenging angel), whereas *revenge* arises from baser motives (the revenge of a jealous lover).

2. *delegate/relegate:* To *delegate* a task is merely to hand it over; to *relegate* it, however, is to place it in a lower position or order of priority.

3. *deplore/deprecate:* If you *deplore* a thing, you regret it. *Deprecate* is the word people used before *put down* entered our vocabulary.

4. *nauseous/nauseated:* Something *nauseous* has the capability to induce nausea. *Nauseated* is the way people feel when they encounter something *nauseous*.

5. *notable/noticeable:* A *notable* difference is one worth noticing; a *noticeable* difference is merely conspicuous.

6. *persistence/perseverance: Persistence* is dogged resolve. It's the interior attitude of which the exterior manifestation is often *perseverance,* that is, continuing in the same path despite difficulties.

7. *pervade/permeate:* When someone closes a window and puts a match to a pile of oily rags, the smell soon *pervades:* It's soon present throughout the room. If that smell is to make its way to the next room, however, it has to *permeate,* or pass through, a barrier.

8. *presume/assume:* If you *assume* I'll come to your party, it's because you have already made up your mind that I will, or because I have some obligation to show up. But if you *presume* I'll come, you're taking me for granted and will be surprised if I don't come.

3-24. More Confusables

1. Although these words are often used interchangeably, the distinction should be maintained: *To imply* means "to express something indirectly to someone"; *to infer* means "to draw a conclusion from something."

   During my interview with the vice president, I **inferred** that she was looking for someone with more experience.

2. See the explanation for item 1.

   The author **implied** in the preface that the reclusive rock star had authorized the publication of this exclusive biography.

3. A *disinterested* person is neutral or unbiased; an *uninterested* person lacks interest. Therefore, mediators may or may not be *uninterested* in an event or an activity, but they must be *disinterested* to do a good job.

   The best kind of mediator is one who is **disinterested** in the outcome.

4. Circumstances or things may be *adverse* (difficult or unpleasant to endure), but the person who is reluctant to endure perceived hardship is said to be *averse* to it.

   My guests were so **averse** to political discussion that I steered the conversation away from talk of the election.

Continued on next page

5. Most dictionaries label *to enthuse* as colloquial or substandard for "to be enthusiastic" or "to show enthusiasm for."

   The author was enthusiastic about the possibility that a producer might purchase film rights to his novel.

6. The word *healthy* is often used incorrectly. *Healthy* means "having health," and *healthful* means "giving health." Therefore, animals and people are *healthy*; foods, activities, and climates are *healthful*.

   Because the climate in Arizona is so healthful, the doctor suggested that her patient recuperate there.

7. To *flaunt* is to show off or proudly display something; to *flout* is to scorn or ignore a convention or rule.

   Nudists flout no laws when they flaunt their physiques on Greek beaches.

8. A disbelieving or skeptical person is *incredulous*; an unbelievable thing or event is *incredible*.

   The incredulous prosecuting attorney pressed the defendant for more details about the day in question.

9. In *The Careful Writer*, Theodore Bernstein has one thing to say about the word *irregardless*: "illiterate." Always follow *regardless* with a prepositional phrase.

   Regardless of the outcome of the merger, all employees were guaranteed their jobs and their benefits.

10. Both words mean "capable of being easily ignited and of burning quickly"; however, because *inflammable* may be misinterpreted to mean "not flammable," *flammable* is the more acceptable of the alternatives.

    For consumer protection, a fuel company in Florida now labels its products "flameable" instead of flammable.

CHAPTER 4
WRITING AND REWRITING

- in my personal opinion

- in the not-too-distant future

- for the purpose of explaining

- Hopefully, the measures will be adopted.

- the marketing department strategy committee formation meeting

- neither his attitude nor what he accomplished

All good writing involves rewriting. This chapter deals with ways of tightening your prose to make it clearer and more effective by eliminating wordiness, nonparallel constructions, smothered verbs, and noun strings.

The chapter also encourages you to recognize clichés, jargon, and fuzzy language in general so you can avoid them and keep your writing fresh and readable.

4-1. Breaking the Wordiness Habit

Can you cut the following fillers down to size?

1. in this day and age
2. it is incumbent on me
3. following after
4. 2 o'clock in the afternoon
5. for the price of $50
6. to the fullest possible extent
7. advance warning
8. in my personal opinion
9. enclosed herewith
10. merge together
11. bring to a conclusion
12. contained on
13. make an assumption that
14. it is recommended that consideration be given to
15. until such time as
16. on the occasion of
17. pursuant to our agreement
18. in view of the fact that, due to the fact that
19. of considerable magnitude
20. within the realm of possibility
21. oval in shape
22. refer back
23. for the purpose of explaining
24. in the not-too-distant future
25. one and the same
26. extend an invitation
27. give authorization for

Answers are on page 181.

Homographs/Homophones/Homonyms

Homographs are words that are spelled alike but are different in meaning, derivation, or pronunciation: the *bow* of a ship, a *bow* and arrow. **Homophones** are words that sound alike but are different in meaning, derivation, or spelling: *to, two, too; course, coarse*. Homophones are often the source of puns. **Homonyms** are words that are spelled and pronounced alike but have different meanings (i.e., they're both homographs and homophones): *rack* (v.) and *rack* (n.).

4-2. Set Verbs Free

Verbs—the powerful words that spin the tales we like to read and hear. What happens to those verbs when bureaucratese takes over? They become smothered—*also called* camouflaged *or* buried. *But whatever you call them, all too often verbs are turned into nouns or adjectives. Empower the following sentences by unburying the verbs. Make any other necessary changes. If a sentence is in the passive and the doer of the action is unknown, use "we" as the subject.*

1. Authorization for the new vacation schedule was given by the project manager.

2. Consideration is being given to your proposal, and if approval is given, an adjustment to the present procedure will be made.

3. We will extend an invitation to all those who made a contribution of their time.

4. We will effect an improvement of the present sick leave policy by making an amendment that will allow employees the use of sick leave, rather than personal leave, for the care of an ill parent.

5. Before the merger between the two companies can occur, officials must be in agreement with the stockholders.

6. After the submission of our entry to the judges, we made the decision to give any winnings to a local charity.

7. The new administrator made reference to the poor organizational skills of his predecessor.

8. The preparation of the new procedural manuals will have to be accomplished by an outside consultant.

9. The review of the cover designs by the graphic artist will reach completion by the close of business today.

Answers are on page 181.

4-3. Redundancies

Redundancies are unnecessary repetitions. Eliminate the redundancies in the following sentences.

1. The undergraduate student hoped to attend graduate school to earn a doctorate degree.

2. Because of her successful achievements in the state legislature, Senator Brown easily defeated the present incumbent for governor.

3. The important essentials of the proposal focused attention on mutual cooperation between our firm and our client.

4. The usual custom is for the new recruits to have a three-month training period, but we will make an exception in this case.

5. Although few in number, the beneficial aspects of the new innovation far outweigh the drawbacks.

6. Hounding by the media forced the heir to the multimillion-dollar estate to seek a private retreat.

7. The past history of the hospital indicates excellent handling of serious crises as well as day-to-day events.

8. The general consensus of opinion was that the passing fad could potentially adversely affect young teenagers.

9. The new manager's future plans include eliminating altogether the good medical and dental benefits now offered to the employees.

10. In order to prereserve your place in the seminar, call this office in advance.

Answers are on page 182.

4-4. Shifts in Construction

Careless shifts in tense, voice, mood, person, or number can distort meaning and confuse readers. In the following sentences, identify the shifts—sometimes called mixed constructions—*and improve the sentences by making inconsistent elements parallel, supplying missing elements, or correcting pronoun-antecedent ambiguity. In some cases, it's better to rewrite the sentence.*

1. If there are no signs of breathing or if no signs of a pulse are evident, take the first step in artificial respiration by placing one hand under the victim's neck and then you should put your other hand on the forehead of the victim so that the forehead can be tilted back.

2. When a victim loses consciousness often scares a rescue worker.

3. Immediately after he accidentally cut his arm, his shirt was soaked with blood. His friend places a clean cloth directly over the wound and presses firmly.

4. If a person is suffering from food poisoning, you may feel the symptoms within a few minutes.

5. If a food poisoning victim has severe symptoms, they should notify a doctor.

6. In the morning, the first-aid students learned about remedies for frostbite; in the afternoon, the Heimlich Maneuver was demonstrated.

7. The tourniquet was a temporary first-aid attempt but which was necessary.

8. The instructor explained that treating a burn with ice or cold water is preferable to when you adhere to the old wives' tale of using butter or oil.

9. Anyone can learn CPR if you try.

10. The Coast Guard instructor told us not to transport a drowning victim to shore first but that we should begin CPR while the victim is in a boat or floating in the water.

Answers are on page 183.

4-5. Problems with Parallelism I

According to Words Into Type, *parallelism is "the principle that parts of a sentence that are parallel in meaning should be parallel in structure." Can you make these sentences parallel?*

1. The publisher will either send the galleys by courier or by express mail.

2. The responsibilities of the new secretary included answering the telephone, greeting new clients, and to take minutes at the staff meetings.

3. The software package I reviewed is inefficient, presents complications, and it is overpriced.

4. The magazine article discussed the following topics:

    a. What you should know about buying a new car

    b. How to lease a car

    c. Applying for a car loan

    d. The choice between a foreign-built and an American-built car

5. After Sarah and James announced their engagement, they not only hoped for their parents' approval but also their blessing.

6. The across-the-board raises were approved both by the manager and the vice president.

7. The committee concluded that the sick leave policy should be changed, having office parties should be done less elaborately, and all employees should be asked their opinions about a four-day work week.

8. Did you inform your editors about the change in number style by the client and that the client has shortened our deadline by two days?

9. Understanding the facts about the situation is to know the truth.

10. A survey revealed that 90 percent of the employees favor a smoke-free workplace, and three-fourths of the employees would work overtime to meet a deadline, and some of the employees feel office morale needs to be improved.

Answers are on page 185.

Half-Dead Precisionist

Before publishing the now classic *Elements of Style* by Strunk and White, White's editor at Macmillan sent some copies to teachers of English composition, asking for comment. The main criticism was that Strunk and White were too prescriptive; the recommendation was that the book be brought "more in tune" with modern educational theory, the substance of which seemed to be that any usage could be considered acceptable and correct, as long as it had currency and didn't offend against taste. On being informed that Macmillan thought that he should bring the book more in line with the "demands of the market," White replied:

I was saddened by your letter—the flagging spirit, the moistened finger in the wind, the examination of entrails, and the fear of little men. I don't know whether Macmillan is running scared or not, but I do know that this book is the work of a dead precisionist and a half-dead disciple of his, and that it has got to stay that way.... I know that I cannot, and will-shall not, attempt to adjust the unadjustable Mr. Strunk to the modern liberal of the English Department, the anything-goes fellow. Your letter expresses contempt for this fellow, but on the other hand you seem to want his vote. I am against him, temperamentally and because I have seen the work of *his* disciples, and I say the hell with him. If the White-Strunk opus has any virtue, any hope of circulation, it lies in our keeping its edges sharp and clear, not in rounding them off cleverly....

—From *E.B. White: A Biography*, by Scott Elledge (New York: Norton, 1986)

4-6. Problems with Parallelism II

The long sentences that follow lack parallel construction. Generally speaking, a sentence should be no longer than about 20 words, for after this point the reader begins to lose interest. However, even a long sentence can become easy to read if the writer uses parallel construction.

In addition to correcting the following nonparallel constructions, make any other improvements you can to these sentences.

1. Last week's drive through the Rocky Mountains reminded Lisa of Switzerland with its snowcapped peaks and picturesque mountain villages and of what a wonderful time she spent with relatives whom she had never met before.

2. The writings of Charles Dickens were greatly affected by the hardships of his miserable childhood and that he spent years observing and writing about crime and poverty in the streets of London while he was a newspaper reporter.

3. Homer's *Odyssey* relates the wanderings of Odysseus after the Trojan War, Odysseus's fighting with giants, conflicts with magical maidens, Odysseus's miraculous escape from monsters, and how he safely arrived back home.

4. The new, easy-to-read book on report writing treats writing as part of a communication system involving the writer, the editor, and the reader, by breaking down the writing process into interrelated steps that should be completed in a specific order; that those who need to write reports in their fields of specialization can do so with an efficient step-by-step approach; and the book used many examples from actual drafts and published reports.

5. Jargon is sometimes used in an in-house memo, but generally writers should avoid jargon in reports, but they have found when gearing a report to a specific group of readers, that it is necessary to use the private language of the group to show that they are familiar with the group's particular field.

Answers are on page 188.

4-7. Problems with Parallelism III

Rework or rewrite the following sentences to correct errors in parallelism that interrupt the flow and cloud the meaning.

1. The boss told him to stop acting like a disgruntled employee and not undermining the office morale.

2. Neither his attitude nor what he accomplished will make any difference to me.

3. Every day when she sat at her desk, she was absorbed in her work, totally unaware of other employees, and everyone saw how completely happy she was.

4. Who can ever forget his generosity and that he contributed to saving the organization?

5. She discussed the causes as well as giving the ramifications of the project's editorial problems.

6. It appears that no matter what he does or all the ways he tries, he still has trouble making his car run properly.

7. Jack is a proofreader who is fast, accurate, and has capability.

8. You can gain your objective at this point by biding your time and the development of your skills.

9. Cooking is a delightful hobby, but to eat all the results can be fattening.

10. She can get better results by cooperating with the staff than if she demands their services.

Answers are on page 189.

4-8. Noun Strings

When confronted with long strings of nouns that act as modifiers, readers struggle to figure out what the "real" noun is. NTC's Handbook for Writers *(Lincolnwood, IL: NTC Business Books/Contemporary Publishing Group, 1995) says that readers are forced to read such strings backward—from right to left—to understand the relationships among the parts. Some nouns act as compound adjectives, while one or more nouns may independently modify the main noun. Like beads on a string, such nouns lose their distinction.*

In Error-Free Writing: A Lifetime Guide to Flawless Business Writing *(Englewood, Cliffs, NJ: Prentice Hall, 1995), Robin A. Cormier notes that "eliminating noun strings usually creates slightly longer sentences, but the additional words help the reader grasp the meaning more quickly."*

For example, computer programs advance information *could be rewritten as* information about advances in computer programs. *Adding hyphens to compound modifiers can also clarify their relationship, as in* leash–law–abiding citizens, *but it's generally better to recast the sentence. To break strings up into more manageable pieces, rewrite by using these techniques:*

- start at the end of a noun string and work backwards

- create short prepositional phrases

- change nouns into verbals or verbs

Try your hand at rewriting the noun strings below.

1. The marketing department strategy committee formation meeting was changed to 2 P.M.

2. The company offered a new temporary employee orientation seminar.

3. The bond loss deduction carry-forward limitation provision has expired.

4. We reviewed the sample disaster related funding allocation request.

5. The artisan displayed different formula fine molten glass strands.

6. The bank specializes in community banking funds transfer risk management.

7. This is the new Spanish speaking mental health research center.

8. The fiscal year 1996 Bailey Seaton Hospital uniform treatment agreement was ratified after intensive negotiations.

9. Oklahoma Natural Gas Company Employee Counseling Program survey respondents said they thought that the counselors were effective.

10. Elderly problem drinker programs are opening nationwide.

Answers are on page 190.

On High School Students and Real Estate Taxes

The *United States Government Printing Office Style Manual* has a good rule for using hyphens with noun strings: "Where meaning is clear and readability is not aided, it is not necessary to use a hyphen to form a temporary or made compound. Restraint should be exercised in forming unnecessary combinations of words used in normal sequence." Some examples of strings that need no help:

child welfare plan	*per capita expenditure*
civil rights case	*real estate tax*
high school student	*special delivery mail*
income tax form	

4-9.   Rewriting for Clarity I

Try to improve this paragraph, which was taken from an article published in the New York Times. You'll find comma faults, odd word choice, illogical emphasis, misplaced modifiers, and more. Hint: Remember that a company can't be an it *and a* who *in the same place at the same time.*

Napp Technologies, the company whose chemical plant exploded and killed four workers last week, is gone from Lodi for good. Bowing to pressure from an angry community and restrictive zoning, Napp said today that it will not rebuild its plant in Lodi. "Given the extent of the damage, and land use constraints, it will not be feasible to rebuild at our present location," said Napp's president, Hans Peter Kirchgaessner, in a statement released by the company's public relations firm. Mr. Kirchgaessner's statement said that Napp "would not impose our presence on any community or build where we are not wanted." Napp pledged to do everything within its power to help the 106 surviving employees of the plant, which manufactured chemicals for pharmaceuticals and cosmetics.

Answers are on page 190.

4-10.   Rewriting for Clarity II

The following sentences are grammatically correct but awkward; all would benefit from being rewritten.

1.   It is I who am responsible for the errors in the catalog.

2.   The bases of their complaints are lack of good management, lack of proper quality control, and lack of an up-to-date employee benefit package.

3.   The family are going on their vacations this week.

4.   The two-, three-, and four-sided, -angled, and -colored sculptures drew quite a bit of attention at the local fair.

5.   Several people met their deaths during the rampage of Hurricane Andrew.

6. There were findings that should have been more thoroughly researched by the scientists before being presented as conclusive.

7. Each of the engineers had earned himself/herself an enviable reputation by his/her research.

8. When the dog lets go of the sock, throw it in the trash.

Answers are on page 192.

Elusive Quantities

Precision isn't always possible in attempting to describe research results when numbers aren't used. If you read that one dog food won *a majority* of the votes in one market test and another won *most* of the votes in another, which would you say received a higher percentage? Although it's clear that *a majority* is more than 50 percent, what constitutes *a large majority* or *a substantial majority*?

In an effort to answer such questions, Response Analysis of Princeton, New Jersey, has constructed the following guidelines:

Descriptor	Percentage Equivalent
All	100%
Nearly all	90% or more
Most	80% or more
A (large, vast, substantial) *majority*	75% or more
A majority	51% or more
A (bare, slight) *majority*	51% to 55%
Half	50%
Almost or *about half*	46% to 54%
A minority	Less than 50%
A (large, substantial) *minority*	40% to 49%
A plurality	The largest percentage among groups under 50%

4-11. Fraudulent Terms*

Match each devious term with its definition.

Fraudulent Terms

1. unique retail biosphere
2. immediate consumption channel
3. thermal soil remediation unit
4. temporarily displaced inventory
5. synthetic glass
6. normal gratitude
7. positive restructuring
8. mental activity at the margins
9. thermal therapy kit
10. misconnect rate

What They Really Mean

a. bankruptcy

b. stolen goods

c. bribe

d. incinerator

e. bag of ice cubes

f. insanity

g. lost luggage

h. plastic

i. farmers' market

j. soda vending machine

*Adapted from *The New Doublespeak*, by William Lutz (New York: HarperCollins, 1996).

Answers are on page 194.

Answers are on page 194.

Oddment

The word *jargon* used to mean the song of birds, and now it means the song of doctors, lawyers, coaches, psychologists, dope addicts, and professors of English....Jargon is special language used by a group. Its main concern is to save time, to enable the group to speak of its own concerns in a swift, precise way...[and] to promote the solidarity and interests of the group by means of secret language. Jargon becomes a problem when it escapes from the group and other people start using it. When that happens, the words begin to lose whatever meaning they had....The more popular the jargon, the likelier it is to be some kind of stamp....Anytime we label a person's thought or character, we resort to jargon....I'm not being fussy in warning you away from jargon. A good writer never touches it.

—Robert C. Pinckert, *Pinckert's Practical Grammar* (Cincinnati: Writer's Digest Books, 1986)

4-12. Bugaboos

Tap any group of editors or writers and most will unhesitatingly volunteer an idiosyncratic list of meaningless or mindlessly misused words that really bug them.

In an October 31, 1994, article by a Wall Street Journal *editor, Ned Crabb, three of the worst in his list of "words that go bump in the night" are* lifestyle *("Did Abraham Lincoln have a lifestyle?"),* caregiver *(What happened to* mother, father, physician, nurse?*), and* signage *(as in* signs*). But obviously he has a much longer list he can only hint at:*

> Enabler words that have impacted and empowered us, but which could resonate negatively on our spiritual wellness and make us dysfunctional, despite nurturing parenting. But we must not cave; we must prioritize and confront, and synergize a new modality that we can utilize, macrodimensionally, to heal through proactive mentoring.

To a Washington Post *editorial writer (November 2, 1994), it's* gentleman, *as in "The gentleman was last seen wearing a ski mask and firing at random from a pickup truck on I-63."*

To Jacques Barzun, the list of inanities is practically endless (seven tightly packed pages in the Autumn 1994 American Scholar*). His nominations include*

- addressed *("Everything these days is addressed instead of being* dealt with, discussed, stated, mentioned, defined, taken up, met, treated, acknowledged, recognized, settled by the court, taken care of, resolved")

- parenting *(instead of rearing, raising, bringing up, nurturing, caring for, training, cherishing, or perhaps merely being a parent)*

- concerted *(when used to refer to an effort made by one person rather than several* in concert*)*

- format *(when used not of books but about the details or arrangements of a conference or a picnic)*

- *"all those smart words ending in* –ize, *from* finalize, personalize, *and* prioritize *to such ad hoc formations as* Mirandize *(read the suspect his rights)"*

At the top of many lists of bugaboos is hopefully *because the word, used as a sentence adverb (as in "Hopefully, the measures will be adopted"), provokes an unreasoning response. The long usage note in* The American Heritage Dictionary of the English Language, *3rd edition (AHD) explains the problem best. After acknowledging the analogy to* mercifully *and* frankly, *the note says that although opposition to this use of* hopefully *might have been expected to subside over time, in fact, the more*

Continued on next page

some people use hopefully, *the more other people object to it. Indeed, support for this use of* hopefully *among members of* AHD's *Usage Panel fell from 44 percent in 1969 to 27 percent in 1992, despite recognition that there is no precise substitute. The dictionary concludes:*

> It seems that this use of *hopefully* has been made a litmus test, which distinguishes writers who take an active interest in questions of usage from the great mass of people who keep their own linguistic counsel.

Also high up on some bugaboo lists are the following:

- commit, *as in "About 9,000 fewer donors committed to give this year"* (Washington Post, *May 22, 1994)*

- –containing, *as in* caffeine–containing products *(*Washington Post, *November 2, 1994)*

- summit, *as in reference to any gathering of three or more people to discuss any subject*

- the individual, *as in* the gentleman *wearing the ski mask above*

- to grow the economy, to involve the parents, *and* to impact our future, *as in recent political pronouncements*

- dilemma, *instead of* problem *(a dilemma is a special situation to which all the solutions are equally undesirable)*

Now try your hand at replacing or deleting the following bugaboos:

1.	additionally	9.	for a period of four years
2.	as such	10.	have to, has to, needs to
3.	assure an outcome	11.	hopefully
4.	concerning, regarding	12.	impact the proposal
5.	the reason is because	13.	individuals
6.	etiology	14.	is knowledgeable of
7.	FAX	15.	methodology
8.	firstly, secondly, lastly	16.	on the part of

17. prior to

18. several disparate

19. symptomatology

20. to the maximum extent

Answers are on page 194.

21. towards, afterwards

22. transpired

23. utilize, –ing, –ation

The Fuzzy *With*

As a preposition, *with* has well over a score of distinguishable meanings, but inexperienced writers often use the word loosely.

With is sometimes used as a kind of tow-chain to attach to a sentence a thought that would be treated more clearly and grammatically as an independent clause following either a semicolon or *and*. Example: "English and history are his majors, *with* a minor in economics." Better: "...; his minor is economics."

H.W. Fowler (*A Dictionary of Modern English Usage*) suggests that *with* came into popular usage to replace *as to* and *in the case of*. Example: "With pipes, as with tobacco, William Bragge was one of the most successful collectors."

Jacques Barzun (*Simple & Direct*, New York: Harper & Row, 1985) gives an example in which *with* strays from the literalness of "Come with me" to a more elliptical meaning: "With her relatives gone, she could start her housework." Better: "Without her relatives,..."

Another of Barzun's examples points to the error of ascribing to *with* the conjunctive power of *and*. In the book jacket blurb "...married *with* two children," the preposition *with* has been substituted for more than one word and more than one part of speech. Better: "...married, Smith has two children."

The editorial solution is to query the "withness" of the *with*. In the sentence "Most of the victims were older, *with* ages ranging from 55 to 65," what is *with* what? Nothing is *with* anything. Substitute *their* for *with*.

4-13.   A Potpourri of Pesky Problems

Here are some of the problems that seem to give writers and editors the most trouble. Complete the sentences and check your choices against the answers.

1. One of the (principles/principals) of the firm (ensured/assured) me that the (principles/principals) on which the organization was founded remain the same and that the (principle/principal) concern remains protecting the stockholders' equity and adding to their (principle/principal).

2. You can be (ensured/assured) that I in turn will (insure/assure) the stockholders that the firm will (insure/ensure) that no publicity will accompany the transition and that policies to (insure/ensure) the firm's basic solvency will be in place.

3. According to the polls, a majority of the voters (prefers/prefer) one of the two front-running candidates, but what will happen if none of the three contenders (wins/win) decisively in November?

4. The opposition (has continuously/continuously has) tried to subvert the government's fiscal and political reforms to the extent that the country is on the brink of collapse.

5. He collapsed in his office (due to/from) an apparent heart attack, but subsequent tests revealed that his collapse was (due to/caused by) a stroke.

6. A contemporary of my (uncle's/uncle) survived three years in a prisoner-of-war camp in the Philippines.

7. Mickle and Ivey (1995) (asserts/assert) in their report on changes in the workplace that the current downsizing trend has bottomed out.

8. A few of the cities studied—(i.e./e.g.), San Francisco and Dallas— show a decided upturn in their growth indexes and other indicators— (i.e./e.g.), housing starts, unemployment rate, and business tax rates.

9. Whether inflation will be controlled and whether the stock market will rebound at the end of the year (remains/remain) to be seen.

10. If she (was/were) hoping to make a good impression, she didn't prepare adequately.

Answers are on page 195.

4.1 Breaking the Wordiness Habit

1. today *or* now	15. when, until
2. I must	16. on, for, when
3. after	17. as we agreed
4. 2:00 P.M.	18. because, since
5. for $50	19. large
6. fully	20. possible
7. warning	21. oval
8. in my opinion *or* I think	22. refer
9. enclosed	23. to explain
10. merge	24. soon, next week, tomorrow, *or* a specific date
11. conclude	
12. on	25. the same
13. assume that	26. invite
14. please consider	27. authorize

4-2. Set Verbs Free

Many correct answers are possible. The following sentences present some of them:

1. The project manager authorized the new vacation schedule.

2. We are considering your proposal, and if we approve it, we will adjust the present procedure.

3. We will invite all those who contributed their time.

4. We will improve the present sick leave policy by amending it so that employees can use sick leave, rather than personal leave, to care for an ill parent.

Continued on next page

5. Before the two companies can merge, officials and stockholders must agree.

6. After we submitted our entry to the judges, we decided to give any winnings to a local charity.

7. The new administrator referred to the poor organizational skills of his predecessor.

8. A consultant must prepare the new procedural manuals.

9. The graphic artist will review the cover designs before the close of business today.

4-3. Redundancies

Each sentence has at least one redundancy. Most of the words have been deleted because they're part of the definition of another word in the sentence. For example, in the first sentence, an *undergraduate* is by definition a *student*; therefore, *student* is unnecessary.

1. The undergraduate ~~student~~ hoped to attend graduate school to earn a doctorate ~~degree~~.

2. Because of her ~~successful~~ achievements in the state legislature, Senator Brown easily defeated the ~~present~~ incumbent ~~for~~ governor.

3. The ~~important~~ essentials of the proposal focused ~~attention~~ on ~~mutual~~ cooperation between our firm and our client.

4. The ~~usual~~ custom is for the ~~new~~ recruits to have ~~a three-month~~ three months of training ~~period~~, but we will make an exception in this case.

5. Although few ~~in number~~, the ~~beneficial aspects~~ benefits of the ~~new~~ innovation far outweigh the drawbacks. (The *beneficial aspects* phrase is wordy without being strictly redundant.)

6. Hounding by the media forced the heir to the multimillion–dollar estate to seek a ~~private~~ retreat.

7. The ~~past~~ history of the hospital indicates excellent handling of ~~serious~~ crises as well as day-to-day events.

8. The ~~general~~ consensus ~~of opinion~~ was that the ~~passing~~ fad could ~~potentially~~ adversely affect (or harm) young teenagers. (Keep either *general opinion* or *consensus; consensus* means "general opinion." *Young teenagers* isn't strictly redundant; subsets of older teens can be distinguished from younger ones.)

9. The new manager's ~~future~~ plans include eliminating ~~altogether~~ the ~~good~~ medical and dental benefits now offered to the employees.

10. ~~In order~~ To ~~pre~~reserve your place in the seminar, call this office ~~in advance~~.

4-4. Shifts in Construction

There are several possible solutions. Here are a few:

1. The compound dependent clauses lack parallel structure; the independent clauses shift from the imperative to the indicative mood.

   If there are no signs of breathing or there is no pulse, you should take the first step in artificial respiration: Place one hand under the victim's neck and then put the other hand on the victim's forehead and tilt the head back.

   Or

   If no pulse or signs of breathing are evident, take the first step in artificial respiration by placing one hand under the victim's neck and then putting the other hand on the victim's forehead and tilt the head back.

2. An adverb clause is trying to serve as the subject of the sentence.

   When a victim loses consciousness, a rescue worker often becomes scared.

   Or

   A victim's loss of consciousness often scares a rescue worker.

Continued on next page

3. The tenses shift needlessly from the first to the second sentence. The action is all sequential, and the same tense should be used throughout.

   Immediately after he accidentally cut his arm, his shirt was soaked with blood. His friend placed a clean cloth directly over the wound and pressed firmly.

   Or

   Immediately after he accidentally cuts his arm, his shirt is soaked with blood. His friend places a clean cloth directly over the wound and presses firmly.

4. The sentence shifts from third person to second. Use one or the other consistently in both the dependent and independent clauses or rewrite the sentence.

   If you are suffering from food poisoning, you may feel the symptoms within a few minutes.

   Or

   Persons who suffer from food poisoning may feel the symptoms within a few minutes.

5. The sentence shifts in number from singular in the dependent clause to plural in the independent clause.

   If a food poisoning victim has severe symptoms, he or she should notify a doctor.

   Or

   A food poisoning victim who has severe symptoms should notify a doctor.

6. The sentence shifts awkwardly from active to passive voice.

   In the morning, the first-aid students learned about remedies for frostbite; in the afternoon, they saw a demonstration of the Heimlich Maneuver.

7. The predicate nominative shifts from a noun to an adjective clause.

   The tourniquet was a temporary but necessary first-aid attempt.

   Or

   The tourniquet was a temporary first-aid attempt, but one that was necessary.

8. The subject of the first dependent clause is a gerund, and the subject of the second dependent clause shifts to *you*.

   The instructor explained that treating a burn with ice or cold water is preferable to adhering to the old wives' tale of using butter or oil.

9. The sentence shifts from third person to second.

   Anyone can learn CPR if he or she tries.

   Or

   You can learn CPR if you try.

10. The sentence shifts from a noun infinitive phrase to a noun clause. Use either phrases or clauses.

    The Coast Guard instructor told us not to transport a drowning victim to shore first but to begin CPR while the victim is in a boat or floating in the water.

    Or

    The Coast Guard instructor told us that we should not transport a drowning victim to shore first but that we should begin CPR while the victim is in a boat or floating in the water.

4-5. Problems with Parallelism I

There are many ways to make these sentences parallel. Some possibilities are offered below.

1. The same grammatical structure that follows *either* must follow *or*.

   The publisher will send the galleys either by courier or by express mail.

   Or

   The publisher will either send the galleys by courier or send them by express mail.

Continued on next page

Or

The publisher **either will send** the galleys **by** courier **or will send** them **by** express mail.

Or just delete *either*.

2. Gerunds and infinitives aren't parallel. Choose either gerund phrases (as follows) or infinitives.

   The responsibilities of the new secretary included **answering** the telephone, **greeting** new clients, and **taking** minutes at the staff meetings.

3. It helps to recast this sentence by using only adjectives after the verb.

   The software package I reviewed is **inefficient, complicated, and overpriced**.

4. Use the same structure in all list items; in this case, each item begins with a gerund.

   The magazine article discussed the following topics:

   a. **Buying** a new car

   b. **Leasing** a car

   c. **Applying** for a car loan

   d. **Choosing** between a foreign-built and an American-built car

5. Use the same grammatical structure following *not only* and *but also*.

   After Sarah and James announced their engagement, they hoped for **not only their parents'** approval **but also their** blessing.

   Or

   After Sarah and James announced their engagement, they hoped **not only for their parents'** approval **but also for their** blessing.

   Or

   After Sarah and James announced their engagement, they **not only hoped for their parents'** approval **but also hoped for their** blessing.

6. Use the same grammatical structure following *both* and *and*.

   The across-the-board raises were approved **by both** the manager **and** the vice president.

   Or

   The across-the-board raises were approved **both by** the manager **and by** the vice president.

7. Items in a series should be in the same grammatical form: words, phrases, dependent clauses, or independent clauses. One solution is to cast the sentence as a series of clauses. (Note that the relative conjunction *that* should be repeated because it links the series of clauses to the verb *concluded*.)

   The committee concluded **that** the sick leave policy **should be changed, that** office parties **should be done** less elaborately, and **that** all employees **should be asked** their opinions about a four-day work week.

8. A prepositional phrase and a dependent clause aren't parallel.

   Did you inform your editors that the client **has changed** the number style and **has shortened** our deadline by two days?

   Or, to avoid repeating the auxiliary *has*, rewrite the sentence:

   Did you inform your editors about the client's **changing** the number style and **shortening** our deadline by two days?

9. Phrases before and after a form of *to be* should have the same grammatical structure.

   Understanding the facts about the situation is **knowing** the truth.

   Or

   To understand the facts about the situation is **to know** the truth.

10. Fractions, percentages, and indefinite pronouns like *some* shouldn't be mixed in a series.

    A survey revealed **that 90 percent** of the employees favor a smoke-free workplace, **that 75 percent** of the employees would work overtime to meet a deadline, and **that [give percentage]** of the employees feel office morale needs to be improved.

4-6. Problems with Parallelism II

There are many acceptable ways to rewrite these sentences; these are some possible solutions.

1. The two prepositional phrases beginning with *of* are connected by the coordinate conjunction *and*; therefore, the same form for the object of the preposition must follow *of*. A noun phrase and a noun clause aren't parallel.

    Last week's drive through the Rocky Mountains reminded Lisa of Switzerland with its snowcapped peaks and picturesque mountain villages and of the wonderful time she spent with relatives whom she had never met before.

2. A prepositional phrase and a noun clause aren't parallel.

    The writings of Charles Dickens were greatly affected by the hardships of his miserable childhood and by the years he spent observing and writing about crime and poverty as a London newspaper reporter.

3. This series is composed of one gerund phrase, three noun phrases, and one clause. They aren't parallel. Each item in the series should be in the same form: Noun phrases might be best. Also, to avoid repeating Odysseus's name, use it once in the main clause and then use a colon before the list.

    Homer's *Odyssey* relates the many experiences of Odysseus after the Trojan War: his travels from place to place, his fights with giants, his conflicts with magical maidens, his miraculous escape from monsters, and his safe arrival home.

4. Although this sentence could easily be corrected by breaking it into several sentences, it can be made more digestible by using a series of verb phrases.

    The new, easy-to-read book on report writing treats writing as part of a communication system involving the writer, the editor, and the reader; breaks down the writing process into interrelated steps that should be completed in a specific order; offers writers in specialized fields an efficient step-by-step approach; and uses many examples from actual drafts and published reports.

5. This sentence shifts its focus from *jargon* to *writers* to *it* as the subject; the verb tense also shifts. Here's one solution.

Although jargon is often acceptable for in-house memos, writers generally avoid using it in reports; however, many writers have found that, when gearing a report to a specific group, they must use the private language of that group to show familiarity with a particular field.

4-7. Problems with Parallelism III

1. The boss told him to stop acting like a disgruntled employee and undermining the office morale.

2. Neither his attitude nor his accomplishments will make any difference to me.

3. Every day when she sat at her desk, she was absorbed in her work, totally unaware of other employees and completely happy.

4. Who can ever forget his generosity and his contribution to saving the organization?

5. She discussed the causes and ramifications of the project's editorial problems.

6. It appears that no matter what he does or how he tries, he still has trouble making his car run properly.

7. Jack is a fast, accurate, and capable proofreader.

8. You can gain your objective at this point by biding your time and developing your skills.

9. Cooking is a delightful hobby, but eating all the results can be fattening.

10. She can get better results by cooperating with the staff than by demanding their services.

4-8. Noun Strings

Here are some possible answers:

1. The meeting on forming a strategy committee for the marketing department was changed to 2 P.M.

2. The company offered an orientation seminar for new temporary employees.

3. The limitation on carrying forward deductions for bond losses has expired.

4. We reviewed the sample request for an allocation of disaster-related funds.

5. The artisan displayed fine strands of molten glass made from different formulas.

6. The bank specializes in managing the risks involved in transferring community banking funds.

7. This is the new center for research on mental health; all staff members speak Spanish.

8. The fiscal 1996 agreement on uniform treatment at Bailey Seaton Hospital was ratified after intensive negotiations.

9. Survey respondents said they thought that counselors for the Employee Counseling Program at the Oklahoma Natural Gas Company were effective.

10. Programs targeting problem drinkers among seniors are opening nationwide.

4-9. Rewriting for Clarity I

Let's look at each sentence individually.

> The company is elsewhere referred to (correctly) as an *it*, and the appositive can be simplified. The phrase *last week* has been moved next to the word it modifies.

Napp Technologies, which owned the chemical plant that exploded last week and killed four workers, is gone from Lodi for good.

Although one can bow to pressure, bowing to restrictive zoning seems strange. *Restrictive zoning* is actually shorthand. We all know what it means, but the revised sentence makes it clearer. The final clause (*which…cosmetics*) was in the last sentence, but the information is needed at the beginning. Putting the clause in the first sentence would make it too long for this particular lead. Moving the clause made it advisable to make *Lodi* precede the noun, and while *its* could stay, *the* sounds a little better.

In response to pressure from an angry community and changes that made zoning more restrictive, Napp said today that it will not rebuild the Lodi plant, which manufactured chemicals for pharmaceuticals and cosmetics.

In general, direct quotes should be left alone, but here we need to change *our* to *the*—a change we bracketed so that it's clear to the reader that the word wasn't in the original quotation—to match the rest of the article. Changing punctuation, in the form of deleting the unnecessary comma, however, doesn't really change the quotation.

"Given the extent of the damage and land use constraints, it will not be feasible to rebuild at [the] present location," said Napp's president, Hans Peter Kirchgaessner, in a statement released by the company's public relations firm.

The same logic as in the preceding sentence applies to these bracketed changes. *Statement* is redundant.

Mr. Kirchgaessner said that Napp "would not impose [its] presence on any community or build where [it is] not wanted."

Also is a transition that ties the last sentence to what went before, and *within* can be shortened to *in*. It's important to report that 106 of 110 employees weren't killed, and there's a stronger way to say it—a clause is more emphatic than a participle. Finally, the company's commitment to helping survivors is diluted by ending the sentence with routine information about the products it manufactures. That information belongs in an earlier sentence.

Napp also pledged to do everything in its power to help the 106 employees who survived the blast.

4-10. Rewriting for Clarity II

The following are possible rewrites.

1. The verb *am* is correct in this sentence because *who* is the subject and *I* is the antecedent of the pronoun *who*; however, *who am* sounds awkward.

   I am responsible for the errors in the catalog.

   Or

   I am the one who is responsible for the errors in the catalog.

2. The confusion in this sentence results from the variable pronunciation of *bases*. On first reading, a reader would most likely pronounce the word as the plural of *base*, as in *the bases are loaded*, when in fact the word should be pronounced as the plural of *basis*. On second reading, the reader would have no problem. But remember, a reader shouldn't have to read a sentence twice to understand it. A better alternative might be to reverse the sentence or else rewrite.

   Lack of good management, proper quality control, and an up-to-date employee benefit package are the bases of their complaints.

   Or

   Their complaints are based on lack of good management, proper quality control, and an up-to-date employee benefit package.

3. In this sentence the members of the collective noun *family* are functioning individually; that is, each family member is going on a separate vacation. Therefore, the plural *are* is correct. To avoid the awkwardness of the sentence, you could insert the phrase *the members of* and add the word *separate*.

   The members of the family are going on their separate vacations this week.

   If in fact the family is going on vacation together, the sentence should read as follows:

   The family is going on its vacation this week.

   Or

   The family is going on vacation this week.

4. This sentence means that the sculptures had two, three, or four sides; two, three, or four angles; and two, three, or four colors. The suspended hyphens make the sentence very complex. In a case like this, rewrite.

    The sculptures that drew quite a bit of attention at the local fair were multicolored and had from two to four sides and angles.

5. Although the plural noun *deaths* is acceptable, the singular *death* is also correct and somehow more clearly indicates that all the deaths happened at about the same time or as a result of the same circumstances. According to *Words Into Type*, "a singular noun is often used with a plural possessive when only one of the things possessed could belong to each individual." Said another way, people only die once and the phenomenon of death can't be shared.

    Several people met their death during the rampage of Hurricane Andrew.

6. Unless you have a good reason for using *there is, there are, there was,* or *there were*, avoid these constructions, as well as the passive voice.

    The scientists should have researched their findings more thoroughly before presenting them as conclusive.

7. To avoid the awkwardness of the "himself/herself" and "his/her" constructions, recast the sentence in the plural.

    The engineers had earned themselves enviable reputations by their research.

    Note that unlike the example in answer 5, here, if you had referred to earning "an enviable *reputation*," your readers could infer that the engineers shared—as a team—the good reputation. A reputation, unlike a death, can belong to both an individual and a group.

8. Although the pronoun antecedent of the pronoun *it* is *sock*, the sentence seems to suggest that the dog might be thrown in the trash.

    When the dog lets go, throw the sock in the trash.

    Or

    Throw the sock in the trash when one the dog lets go of it.

4-11. Fraudulent Terms

1. i. farmers' market	6. c. bribe
2. j. soda vending machine	7. a. bankruptcy
3. d. incinerator	8. f. insanity
4. b. stolen goods	9. e. bag of ice cubes
5. h. plastic	10. g. lost luggage

4-12. Bugaboos

1. also, too, and, in addition	13. persons
2. (Delete!)	14. knows
3. ensure an outcome	15. method
4. on, about	16. by
5. because, the reason is that	17. before
6. cause	18. several
7. fax	19. symptoms
8. first, second, last	20. as much as possible, as much as we can
9. for four years	21. toward, afterward
10. must, should, ought to	22. happened
11. we hope that	23. use, using, the use of
12. affect the proposal	

4-13. A Potpourri of Pesky Problems

1. One of the **principals** of the firm **assured** me that the **principles** on which the organization was founded remain the same and that the **principal** concern remains protecting the stockholders' equity and adding to their **principal**.

2. You can be **assured** that I in turn will **assure** the stockholders that the firm will **ensure** that no publicity will accompany the transition and that policies to **ensure** the firm's basic solvency will be in place.

Both of these sentences contain the same confusables. According to *The New York Public Library Writer's Guide to Style and Usage (NYPL)*,

> ...To add to the confusion, *principal* also refers to the sum of money (think "capit*al*") on which interest is paid or received. A *principal* is also a leading performer or someone who hires an agent. *Principle* is always used as a noun, meaning rule or tenet....To *assure* someone means to make (someone else) confident about something when the element of doubt is present. Both to *ensure* and to *insure* also mean to make certain of something. Despite the journalistic trend away from the traditional use of to *insure*, most careful writers still prefer *ensure* except to denote the reduction of financial risk.

However, the last *ensure* in the second sentence could just as easily be *insure*. The context is financial, and *policies* is equally ambiguous: It could mean "procedures" or actual insurance policies (perhaps a key person policy).

3. According to the polls, a majority of the voters **prefer** one of the two front-running candidates, but what will happen if none of the three contenders **wins** decisively in November?

Majority is a collective noun that's singular in form but plural in meaning, so the verb should be plural. According to *NYPL*,

> *None* can be used with either a singular verb or a plural verb, but most grammarians and style manuals prefer the plural....In the few cases where *none* means "not one" or "no one," the verb is singular.

In this case, logically the verb must be singular because only one person wins.

Continued on next page

4. The opposition **has continuously** tried to subvert the government's fiscal and political reforms to the extent that the country is on the brink of collapse.

According to *Words Into Type* (*WIT*),

> When an adverb is placed within a verb, it should regularly follow the first auxiliary, not precede it—*may safely be used, will surely come.*

5. He collapsed in his office **from** an apparent heart attack, but subsequent tests revealed that his collapse was **due to** a stroke.

According to *The Gregg Reference Manual*, 8th edition (*Gregg*),

> *Due to* introduces an adjective phrase and should modify nouns. It's normally used only after some form of the verb *to be....*

6. A contemporary of my **uncle's** survived three years in a prisoner-of-war camp in the Philippines.

On the so-called "double possessive," *WIT* notes,

> When the thing possessed is only one of a number belonging to the possessor, both the possessive case and *of* are used.

7. Mickle and Ivey (1995) **assert** in their report on changes in the workplace that the current downsizing trend has bottomed out.

In discussing the placement of text citations, *The Chicago Manual of Style*, 14th edition, notes that in the following example ("Carter and Jones (1980) report findings at variance with the foregoing..."),

> "Carter and Jones," however, refers to the authors themselves and the date of their relevant work is parenthetical.

In the example given, the verb is plural.

8. A few of the cities studied (**e.g.,** San Francisco and Dallas) show a decided upturn in their growth indexes and other indicators (**i.e.,** housing starts, unemployment rate, and business tax rates).

The abbreviation *i.e.* means "namely" and *e.g.* means "for example." However, it's easy to confuse them: Are the "other indicators" listed all or some of them? You'd have to know. Although there's a trend toward using *i.e.* and *e.g.* in running text, careful writers restrict their use to parentheses.

9. **Whether inflation will be controlled and whether the stock market will rebound at the end of the year remain to be seen.**

   The subject of the first sentence is two dependent clauses (*whether... controlled* and *whether...year*) joined by *and*. As with all compound subjects joined by *and*, the verb must be plural.

   If the sentence sounds awkward to you because *remains to be seen* is idiomatic, it might be better to rewrite it.

   It remains to be seen whether inflation will be controlled and whether the stock market will rebound at the end of the year.

10. **If she was hoping to make a good impression, she didn't prepare adequately.**

    Not all *if* clauses take the subjunctive. *Gregg* explains it this way:

    > When an *if* clause states a condition that is *highly improbable, doubtful,* or *contrary to fact*, the verb in the *if* clause requires special treatment....

    None of those conditions applies here, so the verb is in the indicative mood, not the subjunctive.

CHAPTER 5

PERENNIAL PROBLEMS

- The jury is ready to deliver their verdict.

- How do you feel about this Federally-funded program?

- The self taught programmer felt self conscious around his coworkers.

- 10 dogs, six cats, and four geese

- African-American and Asian-American citizens

Everyone who has to put thoughts on paper or on a computer screen has faced the perennial problems tackled in this chapter: making pronouns agree with their antecedents and choosing the appropriate style of capitalization, hyphenation, and numbers. This chapter presents some options to help you make informed decisions—and know which authorities are most likely to support your own judgments.

The chapter also shows you how to avoid bias in your writing, as well as various ways of alphabetizing index entries and detecting errors in Internet addresses.

5-1. Nonsexist Language

For the terms, suggest appropriate alternatives. For the sentences on the next page, replace the sexist wording with a nonsexist term.

Terms

1. businessman, businesswoman

2. chairman, chairwoman

3. coed

4. congressman

5. crewman

6. Dear Sir:

7. enlisted man, enlisted woman

8. fireman

9. Gentlemen:

10. housewife

11. mailman

12. man and wife

13. manpower

14. per man

15. policeman

16. repairman, handyman

Bias-Free Writing

No aspect of English has undergone more scrutiny and revision in recent years than so-called biased writing. Terms that were in general use for centuries have virtually disappeared: the generic *he, postman, actress, flesh-colored* (for pink or beige), *nonwhite, old folks' home, crippled, handicapped, deaf,* and *blind.* People have scrambled to find terms that are acceptable without being convoluted.

A task force of the Association of American University Presses labored for eight years to produce *Guidelines for Bias-Free Writing.* In a discussion of ways to avoid sexism, the authors warn against seeking refuge in *one,* because "a shift to the impersonal third person may...produce a flotilla of *ones*—or a reversion to third-person masculine forms," as in this example:

Corruption exists when *one* illicitly puts *one*'s own interests above those of the people and the ideals *one* is pledged to serve.

Corruption exists when *one* illicitly puts *his* own interests above those of the people and ideals *he* is pledged to serve.

In colloquial usage the authors endorse the "singular *they*" to specify an indefinite pronoun or a "multiple choice" antecedent, as in *Everyone has to carry their own luggage,* but it's important to note that not everyone agrees with this guideline.

17. salesman

18. seaman

19. stewardess

20. trashman

Sentences

1. A doctor should explain medical problems to his patients in laymen's terms.

2. The woman lawyer, Elaine Murphy, wore a stunning Chanel suit and won the case for her client, the defendant.

3. The authoress and poetess Michelle Newman will autograph copies of her new book, which is on display at the mall bookstore.

4. Because the male nurse has a fabulous sense of humor, the pediatrician's patients actually enjoy their trips to the doctor's office.

5. Dedicated artists often neglect their wives and children.

6. An editor is responsible for meeting his deadlines.

Answers are on page 217.

Grammar and Gender

From a chapter called "The Word That Failed," which deals with the history of more than 80 pronouns that have been coined to fill the void of a common-gender pronoun to use in constructions such as "Everybody knew *they* had a long wait ahead":

We cannot legislate new words into existence, and no unified mechanism of prescriptive grammar exists to enforce a rule, should we manage to agree on one.

Furthermore, it is not likely that a new pronoun with ideal characteristics can be devised in the same way we create wonder drugs or market pet food....The challenge to the generic masculine will probably come from a different direction, most likely from a set of alternatives already present in the language rather than an innovation which people must be coaxed or forced to use. Perhaps that set will be the one even now employed by many writers and speakers who wish to be both inclusive and inoffensive, while remaining stylistically unobtrusive: singular *they*, in combination with an occasional *he or she* and, when these choices are stylistically inappropriate, the rephrasing of sentences to eliminate the need for a sex-indefinite pronoun.

—Dennis Baron, *Grammar and Gender* (New Haven: Yale University Press, 1986)

5-2. Agreement between Pronouns and Antecedents

An antecedent is the word to which a pronoun refers. Determine the antecedent of each boldfaced pronoun and correct any pronoun/antecedent agreement errors in the following sentences. (Some sentences may be correct.)

1. Each of the companies has sent **their** proposals to **their** prospective clients.

2. Neither Students Against Driving Drunk nor Mothers Against Drunk Driving will be able to distribute **its** brochures at today's meeting.

3. Each writer should include a list of illustrations with **their** manuscript.

Numbers: To Spell Out or Not?

As the world becomes increasingly technical, writers are devising number styles that make their work easier to read. Fewer people are willing to spell out large numbers at all, because figures are easier to understand and easier to compare than words.

All the standard style manuals recognize the problems that number style poses. As *The Chicago Manual of Style*, 14th edition, says:

> It is difficult if not impossible to be entirely consistent in the use of numbers in textual matter.... Several factors work together to govern the choice between spelling out and using numerals for any particular number. Among them are whether the number is large or small, whether it is an approximation or an exact quantity, what kind of entity it enumerates, and what kind of text it appears in—scientific or technological on the one hand, humanistic on the other.

Similarly, *Words Into Type* comments:

> In deciding whether to use numerals or spell out numbers, the nature of the writing should be considered and literary style distinguished from technical and scientific style....

> As a very broad rule, numbers under 101, round numbers (for example, *about two hundred years ago*), and isolated numbers are expressed in words in general text matter; in scientific and technical writing the rule is to use numerals for all physical measures and for most quantities and qualities of 11 and over.

Another rule of thumb is that when several large numbers appear in the same context the style for the larger numbers governs that for the smaller.

Style guides recognize the problems but leave writers to decide what to do in different contexts. Many complications could be eliminated if writers would forget about spelling out numbers between 10 and 100 (except in special circumstances) and approximate numbers, and treat technical and humanistic text the same.

Numerals can be used for *all* numbers whenever numerals make more sense—particularly for two or more numbers, one of which is higher than nine: *children ages 5, 7, and 13*.

4. A doctor must be aware of the emotional needs of **his** patients.

5. Everyone should submit **their** vacation request by next Friday.

6. The staff are going on **their** vacations during the months of July and August.

7. Neither one of the organizations did as well as **they** had planned.

8. If anyone wants **his** computer repaired, **you** should complete a Request for Repair form.

9. Some of the manuscripts have been typeset, but **they** have not been proofread.

10. Neither Michael nor Emily has sent **their** résumé to prospective employers.

11. The jury is ready to deliver **their** verdict.

12. *Consumer Reports* is publishing **their** annual guide to new and used automobiles.

Answers are on page 219.

5-3. *Chicago's* Number Style

Correct the following sentences according to The Chicago Manual of Style, *14th edition* (Chicago).

1. We expect fifty to sixty people to sign up for the three-day seminar on stress management.

2. For our twenty-fifth anniversary, we made a down payment of 5 thousand dollars on a new home situated on three acres.

3. We hoped the company could function with a budget of $15,000,000 dollars, but we actually need a budget of $17,500,000 million dollars.

Continued on next page

4. During the staff meeting, which began at 10:00 o'clock A.M., we voted by secret ballot on the new flextime policy. The result was as follows: 101 voted yes; twenty-nine voted no.

5. 210 pilots and 362 flight attendants came to the union meeting.

6. 1963 was very difficult for our company: We had to decrease our staff by twenty-six %.

7. Because of the accident, traffic has crawled at the rate of five mph for the past two hours.

8. This week our office spent quite a bit of money for three office repairs: $299.75 to replace the parallel port on the computer, fifteen and a half dollars to buy a ceiling fixture lightbulb, and $178 to rewire the multi-line telephones.

9. Our fund-raising campaign will begin on the first of May and end on the 10th.

10. His new book on youth in America focuses on the differences between teenagers in the nineteen sixties and nineteen seventies and those in the 1980s and 90s.

Answers are on page 220.

Capitalization Rules for Titles of Works

Many people are confused about how to handle the titles of publications in text.

The basic rules that follow apply to the titles of books, journals, newspapers, magazines, newsletters, pamphlets, reports, poems, plays, stories, articles, lectures, and musical works.

- Regular titles are normally rendered in "headline style," which capitalizes the first and last words, all nouns, pronouns, adjectives, verbs, adverbs, and subordinating conjunctions *(if, because, as, that)*.
- Articles *(a, an, the)*, coordinating conjunctions *(and, but, or, for, nor)*, and prepositions (regardless of length) are lowercased. The only exceptions are the first or last word of a title or subtitle.
- The *to* in infinitives should be lowercased.
- Unless it's an acronym, no word in a title should ever be set all in capitals, even it's set that way on the title page of a work.

- In a compound term (other than one with a hyphenated prefix, such as *re-establishment*) that comes at the end of a title, the final element is always capitalized, no matter what part of speech it is. Thus:

A Run-in with Authorities

But

Avoiding a Run-In

—adapted from *The Chicago Manual of Style*, 14th edition

5-4. Capitalization, *Chicago* Style

Correct the capitalization errors in the following sentences according to The Chicago Manual of Style, *14th edition; some sentences are correct.*

1. Malcolm Winchester, the president of winston college, will deliver the college's welcoming address to new students.

2. The discussion between president Jessica March and vice president Jonathan Palen focused on the disbursement of company profits.

3. His 80-year-old grandmother invested thousands of dollars in a land deal that turned out to be worth millions.

4. Please, grandmother, can you give me some advice on my investments?

5. Last night the big dipper and the north star were clearly visible.

6. Drive three miles east, turn left, and drive about one mile north. Our building is on the northwest corner of the intersection of first and maple streets.

7. After visiting relatives on the east coast, we will take a leisurely tour through the south.

8. Conventions will be held in south dakota and upper michigan. Someone suggested the south of france, but that would be too expensive.

9. The state of Iowa has been nicknamed the hawkeye state as well as the food market of the world; washington state is known for its majestic mountains and beautiful scenery.

10. In pittsburgh, pennsylvania, the allegheny and monongahela rivers meet to create the ohio river.

11. We will see lakes michigan and superior during our visit to the northern united states.

12. The 1992 winter olympics were held in albertville, france, in the savoy alps—the so-called roof of europe.

Answers are on page 222.

5-5.   Capitalization, *GPO* Style

The United States Government Printing Office Style Manual (GPO) *lists its capitalization rules in chapter 3, pages 23–33, and offers an alphabetical list, "Guide to Capitalization," in chapter 4, pages 35–61.*

Capitalization in GPO *highlights the words that are most important from the perspective of the federal government. Although the rules may seem somewhat arbitrary, the system does have a pattern. Capitalization indicates power, and often a rule for capitalizing or lowercasing a word is based on a political decision.*

Keep in mind that these rules are often quite confusing. GPO *sometimes offers conflicting information, but try for consistency within a document.*

1. After being lost on interstate 95 for several hours, we finally found state route 23.

2. Although the project was federally funded, it had little effect on employees of the federal government.

3. While walking past the national gallery of art, we heard a sidewalk band strike up the national anthem.

4. Several college presidents, including president I. King Jordan of Gallaudet, submitted reports on their funding concerns to the congressional committee.

5. The mile high city is located in the centennial state.

6. The members of the american medical association committee on education agreed to meet more often; this committee is extremely concerned about trends in education.

7. We decided to tour the eastern region of the country before we head to the deep south to visit relatives.

Answers are on page 224.

5-6. Dashes

*Most people know the difference between a hyphen (-) and an em dash (—).
But what about en dashes (–)? What are they and where do they fit into the mix?*

*Standard stylebooks offer differing opinions on such questions. To maintain
consistency and appropriate style in your work, be sure to check your stylebook and
expand on it if necessary to meet the needs of your particular task or environment.*

These general guidelines are based on The Chicago Manual of Style, *14th
edition:*

- Use em dashes to mark an abrupt change in thought or construction or
  to replace parentheses.

- Use hyphens to break words at the ends of lines or to link the parts of
  ordinary compound words or unit modifiers when necessary for style
  or sense.

- Use en dashes to link ranges of continuous numbers (*pp. 24–35*), to join
  prefixes or suffixes to open compounds (*post–World War II conflicts*), to
  link a pair of open compounds (*New York–Los Angeles flight*), or to join
  two or more hyphenated compounds (*Winston-Salem–Wilkes-Barre
  partnership*).

Mark hyphens, em dashes, and en dashes. Proofreaders use =, $\overset{1}{M}$, *and* $\overset{1}{N}$, *respectively.*

1. The researchers-if I understand correctly-are working with
    laboratory-adapted strains of HIV-1.

2. The Arlington Street People's Assistance Network (A-SPAN) operates
    an emergency winter shelter, which serves 40-50 homeless persons a
    night.

3. Los Angeles-based writer Bebe Moore Campbell-author of *Your Blues
    Ain't Like Mine*, among other works-will be the featured speaker.

4. Why so many errors? It's because some careless writers finish a
    story-or think they have finished it-and never look back.

5. Domestic violence, drug abuse, and budget shortfalls-these are some of
    the issues that the mayor-elect will face.

Continued on next page

6. In the Fort Lauderdale-Pompano Beach market, real estate prices should be skyrocketing-or so I'm hoping.

7. A five-year-old tradition, the library's read-aloud programs are extremely popular. Call 555-1234 for information.

8. To close out the 1998-99 program year, the board will hold its annual meeting June 12-15, 1999. Be sure to complete both sides of the registration form on pages 7-8.

9. The 4,940-ton *Triton* boasted two water-cooled-nuclear-fueled reactors in her 450-foot hull.

10. For our non-CD-ROM users-you know who you are-other options are still available at prices ranging from $39.95-$289.95.

11. Our reservations were confirmed on a New York-Paris flight, but we ended up on a New York-London-Paris flight instead.

12. The North Dakota-South Dakota coalition presented a compelling argument for supporting the favorite son candidate.

Answers are on page 226.

Rules for Using Hyphens

Hyphens link two or more words to form a unit. The hyphens cue the reader and thus help keep the syntax clear. Although hyphenation is often a style decision, some words are found in the dictionary with a hyphen, which has become part of the word. These are "permanent compounds": *one-on-one*, *time-consuming*, *cost-effective*.

A hyphen is also used

- with compound adjectives or unit modifiers such as *long-distance*
- with adjectives and a connecting word such as *tried-and-true*
- with compound numbers and letters that form modifiers such as *twenty-dollar bet*
- with prefixes such as *quasi*, *self*, and *half* (with certain exceptions such as *halfhearted* and *selfish*)
- with prefixes that are normally closed up such as *co*, *non*, and *re* if mispronunciation or ambiguity could result (*recover/re-cover*, *coop/co-op*, *re-creation/recreation*, *un-ionized/unionized*)

A hyphen should *not* be used with compound modifiers if the first element of the modifier is an adverb ending in *-ly* (*minimally equipped*, *definitively rejected*) or if the compound is modified by another adverb (*very well prepared students*, *most ill advised business venture*).

5-7. Hyphenating Compound Words and Phrases I

Decide whether the boldfaced words and phrases should be hyphenated, written as one word (solid), or written as two words. Some words or phrases may be correct as written. The answers are given according to The Chicago Manual of Style, *14th edition (Chicago).*

1. The **well-known** author finally completed his *how to* book about home gardening.

2. The very **well-known** politician was **well-intentioned**, but he was unable to communicate effectively with his constituents.

3. The **decision making** procedures were established after an **all-inclusive** study of the **bookkeeping** department.

4. The **out of season** merchandise was offered to our **two hundred odd** preferred customers.

5. My **brother-in-law** supports the **state-wide** referendum that affects the public schools.

6. The **self taught** computer programmer felt **self conscious** around his **coworkers** who had received formal training.

7. The **eagerly-awaited** exchange of vows finally took place after a lengthy **pre-nuptial** ceremony.

8. The **vice-president** of the university was **non-plussed** by the conflict between the **ex-president** and the new president.

9. The contractor needs **two by six inch** wood strips and **ten, twelve, and fourteen foot** boards to complete the addition to the building.

10. The history class covered information from the **pre-Roosevelt** era to the **post-war** decade.

Answers are on page 227.

5-8.   Hyphenating Compound Words and Phrases II

Would you hyphenate the following compounds? Justify your decision.

1.   carbon dioxide emissions, sodium chloride solution

2.   pro rata assessment, per diem allowance, per capita income, per pupil expenses

3.   large scale project, short term loan, high quality product, low income neighborhood

4.   bluish green sea, sky blue truck, blue green algae

5.   secretary treasurer, city state, soldier statesman

6.   20 mile hike, six year old child

7.   fifth floor apartment, Twentieth Century Limited

8. $20 million project, 50 percent increase

9.   grand jury decision, stock exchange building, bubonic plague outbreak

10.   eye catching decor, interest bearing account

11.   poverty stricken family, hard boiled eggs, poorly equipped kitchen

Answers are on page 230.

5-9. Hyphenating Compound Words and Phrases III

Add hyphens as needed for clarity in these phrases gleaned from newspapers and magazines.

1. top secret military facility

2. government sponsored coverup

3. three by five inch cards

4. planned seven day followup and steppedup inspections

5. over the hill reporter and off the record sources

6. all out battle among the 21 member executive committee

7. seven thousand hundred dollar bills

8. third act problems; first and second act problems

9. stock car racing picture

10. nonexclusive, five year deal

11. a high risk, high return investment

12. long sought after top quark

13. high energy physics facilities

14. chintz bedecked Louis Quatorze suite

15. 30 minute ride in a propeller driven airboat

16. two lane Tamiami Trail

17. well qualified entry level applicants

18. last chance gas station

Continued on next page

19. stiff upperlip style

20. eight inflight engine shutdowns and 16 cabin pressure problems

21. 30 percent fall

22. 12 step recovery and relapse prevention movement

23. strong behind the scenes role

24. 2.5 square mile peninsula

25. a so called open access ruling regarding heavily polluting coal fired plants

26. free market economy approach

27. oak pollen induced rhinitis

28. long term, low dose antiinfective medication regimens

29. Washington born, bred, and educated politician

30. often imitated, never duplicated techniques

31. user friendly, technically advanced software

32. non college bound seniors

33. open, sunblasted prairies

34. macro and microeconomics

Answers are on page 231.

5-10. Alphabetizing Index Entries

Have you ever had trouble locating a name in a telephone directory, especially a name with an abbreviation or acronym in it?

Peggy Smith offers this advice in her book Mark My Words *(Alexandria, VA: EEI Press, 1993):*

> Be sure you understand the difference between the letter-by-letter system (used in dictionaries) and the word-by-word system (used in telephone books). The letter-by-letter system alphabetizes up to the first punctuation mark [or capital letter], disregarding space and hyphens. The word-by-word system alphabetizes up to the first solid word. *[In this system, a space precedes a punctuation mark.]*

Here are examples:

Letter-by-Letter	*Word-by-Word*
Southbridge	*South Fork*
South Fork	*South Port*
Southport	*South River*
South Port	*South Tunnel*
South River	*Southbridge*
South Tunnel	*Southport*

According to The New York Public Library Writer's Guide to Style and Usage *(NYPL),*

> Alphabetization is a simple process for a short index using only subject headings in the English language, but it can become a complex issue when the index entries include symbols, numerals, abbreviations, foreign language characters, and personal names preceded by particles. The treatment of initial articles can also be open to choice....

> [In] the letter-by-letter style, all spaces, hyphens, and apostrophes are ignored; the index heading is treated as a single stream of letters up to the first punctuation mark preceding a modifying element or an inversion.

Try your hand at alphabetizing the following list by each method. In the word-by-word style, place numbers before letters. In the letter-by-letter style, incorporate numbers as if they were spelled out. There's one set of subentries.

Continued on next page

cost-volume–profit relationship

costume design

cost accounting

Costa, Victor

Tankerman Manual

tank trucks

1812 Overture

Boeing passenger aircraft

  747

  767

  727

  737

Edwardian era

D^3 Corporation

D Is for Dog

5-hydroxyindoleacetic acid

hypertension

Henry II

Henry VIII

Henry V

Louis XIV

Louis 14th furniture

1982 annual report

1992 annual report

Macdonald, James

McDonald, James

MacDonald, James A.

Macleod, James A.

St. John's

Saint John

Saint Joan

Ste.-Marie

The Hague

El Greco

Las Vegas

The Kamber Group

Answers are on page 234.

5-11. Catching Errors in Internet Addresses

Internet addresses have been proliferating in publications, and they're not going to go away. Learning a little about their structure can help prevent you from publishing erroneous addresses.

There are two common types of Internet addresses: e-mail addresses and Web addresses. Central to each is the host name, *the name of the computer to which the Web connection must be made or to which the e-mail must be delivered.*

A host name consists of groups of characters separated by periods: eeicom.com, thomas.loc.gov, *or* www.quinion.demon.co.uk, *for example. The characters allowed in the groups are the letters* a *to* z, *the digits* 0 *to* 9, *and the hyphen (which can't appear as the first or last character of a group).*

An Internet e-mail address consists of a user name, an at *sign (@), and a host name. For example, in* president@whitehouse.gov, president *is the user name and* whitehouse.gov *is the host name. User names are generally either combinations of characters derived from a person's name or words indicating what the address is used for.*

A Web address consists of the characters http:// *followed by a host name and often some other information. Web addresses are the most common type of* uniform resource locator *(URL).*

The last part of a Web address, like the first part of an e-mail address, is much less predictable than the host name. The simplest Web addresses stop after the host name; for example, http://web.mit.edu *is the home page for the Massachusetts Institute of Technology, and* http://www.w3.org *is the home page for the World Wide Web Consortium.*

Try your hand at spotting the errors in these Internet addresses.

1. 12345,4321@compuserve.com

2. /s=d.louie/ou1=s56l12h@mhs-fswa.attmail.com

3. Lisa Samuels@acme.com

4. http://www.eeicom.com.eye/

5. http://www.the_times.co.uk

6. http://www/switchboard.com

7. http:\\www.stroud.com\new.html

8. htp:/clever.net/quinion/words/

Answers are on page 236.

5-1. Nonsexist Language

Here are some possible solutions for the terms:

1. business executive, manager, leader, owner, entrepreneur

2. Many style guides recommend using **chairman** when the person holding the office is a man, and **chairwoman** when it's a woman. When you need a neutral term because either a man or woman may hold the office or because the holder prefers an alternative, use **chair**. Other alternatives include **head, leader, presiding officer, moderator, chairperson**.

3. student

4. legislator, member of Congress

5. crew member

6. **Dear Sir or Madam:** *or* To: The Editor, The Director, etc.

7. enlisted member, enlisted person, enlisted personnel, enlistee

8. firefighter

9. **Ladies and Gentlemen:** (Or address the letter to the head of the organization by name and title if known; otherwise, use the title alone, rather than addressing the letter to the organization as a whole.)

10. homemaker

11. mail carrier, letter carrier

12. husband and wife, man and woman, married couple

13. workforce, human resources, personnel

14. per person

15. police officer

Continued on next page

16. **maintenance person, repair person** (specifically, **electrician, plumber, carpenter**, etc.)

17. **salesperson, salesclerk, sales representative, sales agent, sales staff** (if plural)

18. **sailor, crewmember**

19. **flight attendant**

20. **trash collector**

Possible solutions for the sentences:

1. To avoid gender-related problems, try to cast potentially sexist terms in the plural. Also, avoid *layman*.

    Doctors should explain medical problems to their patients in everyday terms (*or* **in lay terms**).

2. Don't use compound nouns like *woman lawyer* or *male nurse* unless there's a legitimate reason for making a distinction according to sex. Avoid describing a woman's appearance or clothing when it's irrelevant to the situation.

    Lawyer Elaine Murphy won the case for her client, the defendant.

3. Avoid feminine suffixes.

    Author and poet Michelle Newman will autograph copies of her new book, which is on display at the mall bookstore.

4. Delete the irrelevant word *male*.

    Because the nurse has a fabulous sense of humor, the pediatrician's patients actually enjoy their trips to the doctor's office.

5. Because some artists are women, avoid using *wives*.

    Dedicated artists often neglect their families.

6. Eliminate the gender-linked pronoun *his*.

    An editor is responsible for meeting deadlines.

5-2. Agreement between Pronouns and Antecedents

In many of these sentences, you can choose between using *his or her* or rewording the sentence. In most cases, rewording is advisable.

1. **Each** of the companies has sent **its** proposals to **its** prospective clients.

   Or

   Each of the companies has sent proposals to prospective clients.

2. Correct as written.

   Neither Students Against Driving Drunk nor Mothers Against Drunk Driving will be able to distribute **its** brochures at today's meeting.

3. Each **writer** should include a list of illustrations with **his or her** manuscript.

   Or

   Writers should include a list of illustrations with **their** manuscripts.

4. A **doctor** must be aware of the emotional needs of **his or her** patients.

   Or

   Doctors must be aware of the emotional needs of **their** patients.

5. **Everyone** should submit **his or her** vacation request by next Friday.

   Or

   All **employees** should submit **their** vacation requests by next Friday.

6. Correct: the members of the staff are acting separately; therefore, the verb must be plural. If the sentence sounds awkward to you, even though it's grammatically correct, reword it:

   The staff **members** are going on **their** vacations during the months of July and August.

   Continued on next page

7. Neither **one** of the organizations did as well as **it** had planned.

8. **Anyone** who wants **his or her** computer repaired should complete a Request for Repair form.

   Or

   All **employees** who want **their** computers repaired should complete Request for Repair forms.

   Or

   If **you** want **your** computer repaired, please complete a Request for Repair form.

9. Correct.

   Some of the **manuscripts** have been typeset, but **they** have not been proofread.

10. Although the closer antecedent is feminine, it would be awkward to use *her* before *résumé*; using *a résumé* avoids the problem.

    Neither **Michael nor Emily** has sent **a** résumé to prospective employers.

11. The **jury** is ready to deliver **its** verdict.

12. *Consumer Reports* is publishing **its** annual guide to new and used automobiles.

5-3. *Chicago*'s Number Style

1. This sentence is correct, because *Chicago* style dictates that whole numbers from one through ninety-nine be spelled out.

   We expect **fifty** to **sixty** people to sign up for the **three**-day seminar on stress management.

2. The rule just stated applies to ordinal as well as cardinal numbers. Isolated references to amounts of money in U.S. currency are spelled out or expressed in figures. If the number is spelled out, so is the unit of currency, and if figures are used, the dollar sign precedes them.

   For our **twenty-fifth** anniversary, we made a down payment of **five thousand dollars** (*or* **$5,000**) on a new home situated on **three** acres.

3. Sums of money that would be cumbersome to express in figures or to spell out in full may be expressed by using the word *millions* or *billions*, accompanied by figures and a dollar sign. Don't use both the dollar sign and the word *dollars*.

   We hoped the company could function with a budget of $15 million, but we actually need a budget of **$17.5 million**.

4. Times of day in even, half, and quarter hours are usually spelled out in text. Never use *o'clock* with *A.M.* or *P.M.* or figures. Numbers applicable to the same category should be treated alike within the same context; don't use figures for some (*101*) and spell out others (*twenty-nine*) (this is the consistency rule).

   During the staff meeting, which began at ten o'clock, we voted by secret ballot on the new flextime policy. The result was as follows: **101** voted yes; **29** voted no.

5. At the beginning of a sentence, any number that would ordinarily be set in figures is spelled out, regardless of any inconsistency this usage may create with other numbers in the sentence.

   Two hundred ten pilots and **362** flight attendants came to the union meeting.

   Alternatively, rephrase to avoid spelling out large numbers.

   A total of 210 pilots and **362** flight attendants came to the union meeting.

6. If it's cumbersome to begin a sentence with the spelled-out number, the sentence should be recast. Percentages are set in figures in both humanistic and scientific copy. The percent sign is used only in scientific or statistical copy, and the word *percent* is used in humanistic copy. Arabic numbers are used with both the percent sign and the word *percent*.

   We found 1963 to be a very difficult year for our company: We had to decrease our staff by **26 percent**.

7. If an abbreviation is used for a unit of measure, the quantity is expressed in figures.

   Because of the accident, traffic has crawled at the rate of 5 mph for the past two hours.

   Continued on next page

8. Fractional amounts of money over one dollar are set in arabic numbers. Whole dollar amounts are set with ciphers after the decimal point when they appear in the same context with fractional amounts. If all the amounts are whole dollars, no ciphers are used.

    This week our office spent quite a bit of money for three office repairs: $299.75 to replace the parallel port on the computer, $15.50 to buy a ceiling fixture lightbulb, and $178.00 to rewire the multiline telephones.

9. *Chicago* style prefers that exact dates be written in the sequence day-month-year without internal punctuation. After an exact date has been used, an elliptical reference to another date in the same month is spelled out.

    Our fund-raising campaign will begin on 1 May 1998 and end on the tenth (*or* on 10 May).

10. Spell out references to particular centuries and decades. If decades are identified by their century, figures are used. Don't use apostrophes for plurals of numbers. For consistency, both parts of the sentence should be the same. The two correct alternatives are as follows:

    His new book on youth in America focuses on the differences between teenagers in the 1960s and 1970s and those in the 1980s and 1990s.

    Or

    His new book on youth in America focuses on the differences between teenagers in the sixties and seventies and those in the eighties and nineties.

5-4. Capitalization, *Chicago* Style

1. Personal titles following a name are lowercased. The proper name of a university or college is capitalized. The words *university* and *college* are lowercased when used as common nouns.

    Malcolm Winchester, the president of Winston College, will deliver the college's welcoming address to new students.

2. Civil, military, religious, and professional titles and titles of nobility are capitalized when they immediately precede a personal name as part of

the name. Capitalize the word *company* only if it's part of the formal name.

The discussion between President Jessica March and Vice President Jonathan Palen focused on the disbursement of company profits.

3. Correct. A family title is lowercased when preceded by a possessive.

    His 80-year-old grandmother invested thousands of dollars in a land deal that turned out to be worth millions.

4. A family title is capitalized when it stands alone or is followed by a personal name.

    Please, Grandmother, can you give me some advice on my investments?

5. The names of constellations are capitalized.

    Last night the Big Dipper and the North Star were clearly visible.

6. The words *north*, *south*, *east*, and *west* are lowercased when they indicate general location or refer to geography. The names of streets are capitalized.

    Drive three miles east, turn left, and drive about one mile north. Our building is on the northwest corner of the intersection of First and Maple Streets.

7. The words *north*, *south*, *east*, and *west* are capitalized when they designate specific regions or are an integral part of a proper name.

    After visiting relatives on the East Coast, we will take a leisurely tour through the South.

8. Proper names of states, regions, and countries are capitalized.

    Conventions will be held in South Dakota and Upper Michigan. Someone suggested the south of France, but that would be too expensive.

9. Generally, lowercase a word indicating a political division of the world, a country, or a state when it precedes the name and capitalize it when it follows. Capitalize nicknames of states.

    The state of Iowa has been nicknamed the Hawkeye State as well as the Food Market of the World; Washington State is known for its majestic mountains and beautiful scenery.

    Continued on next page

10. Proper names of cities, states, and rivers are capitalized, even when a generic term follows more than one proper name.

    In Pittsburgh, Pennsylvania, the Allegheny and Monongahela Rivers meet to create the Ohio River.

11. When a generic term precedes more than one name, the term is capitalized. A term that designates a general location is lowercased.

    We will see Lakes Michigan and Superior during our visit to the northern United States.

12. Names of special events are capitalized. (The names of the four seasons are normally lowercased, however.) The names of cities, countries, and mountains are capitalized. Words introduced by *so-called* are lowercased (and are not placed in quotation marks).

    The 1992 Winter Olympics were held in Albertville, France, in the Savoy Alps—the so-called roof of Europe.

5-5. Capitalization, *GPO* Style

1. This is a perfect example of conflicting information. According to rule 3.9, page 24, *interstate* and *route* are not capitalized: "A common noun used with a date, number, or letter, merely to denote time or sequence, or for the purpose of reference, record, or temporary convenience, does not form a proper name and is therefore not capitalized." However, the "Guide" advises capitalization on page 49 for *Interstate* and on page 55 for *Route*.

   State is capitalized. See rule 3.19, page 26: "The official designations of countries, national domains, and their principal administrative divisions are capitalized only if used as part of proper names, as proper names, or as proper adjectives."

   After being lost on Interstate 95 for several hours, we finally found State Route 23.

2. *Federal Government* is capitalized. See rule 3.19, page 26 (answer 1 above). Also see rule 3.20, page 26: "The similar designations *commonwealth, confederation (federal), government, nation (national), powers, republic,* etc., are capitalized only if used as part of proper names, as proper names, or as proper adjectives."

But the "Guide," page 46, shows that *federally* is always lowercased.

Although the project was federally funded, it had little effect on employees of the Federal Government.

3. The "Guide," page 51, shows that *national* is capitalized only when it is used with a capitalized name and is lowercased at other times.

    While walking past the National Gallery of Art, we heard a sidewalk band strike up the national anthem.

4. Regarding the capitalization of *president*, see rule 3.35, p. 29: "Civil, religious, military, and professional titles, as well as those of nobility, immediately preceding a name are capitalized."

    The "Guide," page 42, shows that when *congressional* is used with a common noun, it is lowercased.

    Several college presidents, including President I. King Jordan of Gallaudet, submitted reports on their funding concerns to the congressional committee.

5. See rule 3.32, page 28: "A fanciful appellation used with or for a proper name is capitalized."

    The Mile High City is located in the Centennial State.

6. *Committee* is capitalized if it's part of a name. See page 41 of the "Guide" because the rules for the capitalization of *committee* are especially confusing.

    The members of the American Medical Association Committee on Education agreed to meet more often; this committee is extremely concerned about trends in education.

7. See rule 3.21, page 27: "A descriptive term used to denote a definite region, locality, or geographic feature is a proper name and is therefore capitalized; also for temporary distinction a coined name of a region is capitalized." But also see rule 3.22, page 27: "A descriptive term used to denote mere direction or position is not a proper name and is therefore not capitalized."

    We decided to tour the eastern region of the country before we head to the Deep South to visit relatives.

5-6. Dashes

1. Em, em, hyphen, hyphen.

    The researchers—if I understand correctly—are working with laboratory-adapted strains of HIV-1.

2. Hyphen, rewrite. Many people wouldn't use an en dash for what's really an approximation, not a true range.

    The Arlington Street People's Assistance Network (A-SPAN) operates an emergency winter shelter, which serves from 40 **to** 50 homeless persons a night.

3. En, em, em.

    Los Angeles–based writer Bebe Moore Campbell—author of *Your Blues Ain't Like Mine,* among other works—will be the featured speaker.

4. Em, em.

    Why so many errors? It's because some careless writers finish a story—or think they have finished it—and never look back.

5. Em, hyphen.

    Domestic violence, drug abuse, and budget shortfalls—these are some of the issues that the mayor-elect will face.

6. En, em.

    In the Fort Lauderdale–Pompano Beach market, real estate prices should be skyrocketing—or so I'm hoping.

7. Hyphen, hyphen, hyphen, hyphen. (Because telephone numbers aren't ranges of continuous numbers, *Chicago* uses a hyphen; some other styles use an en dash instead.)

    A five-year-old tradition, the library's read-aloud programs are extremely popular. Call 555-1234 for information.

8. En, en, en.

To close out the 1998–99 program year, the board will hold its annual meeting June 12–15, 1999. Be sure to complete both sides of the registration form on pages 7–8.

9. Hyphen, hyphen, comma, hyphen, hyphen. Yes, the comma is better than the en dash in this case. Trick question.

The 4,940-ton *Triton* boasted two water-cooled, nuclear-fueled reactors in her 450-foot hull.

10. En, hyphen (or en, in some styles), em, em, the word *to*. Another trick question! Although the en dash in a range of numbers or dates does mean *to*, careful writers and editors avoid using the en dash with the word *from*—and, of course, they also use words in combinations such as *between 1992 and 1994* (Note: never *between...to*).

For our non–CD-ROM users—you know who you are—other options are still available at prices ranging from $39.95 **to** $289.95.

11. En, en, en.

Our reservations were confirmed on a New York–Paris flight, but we ended up on a New York–London–Paris flight instead.

12. En.

The North Dakota–South Dakota coalition presented a compelling argument for supporting the favorite son candidate.

5-7. Hyphenating Compound Words and Phrases I

Chicago distinguishes between temporary and permanent compounds. A temporary compound is composed of an adjective modifying a noun. If the adjective were removed, the noun would retain its original meaning. For example, if the word *master* were removed from the phrase *master wheel,* the meaning of *wheel* would not change.

However, if the word *master* were removed from *masterpiece, piece* couldn't stand alone and retain its meaning in the compound. Therefore, temporary compounds are printed as two words, and permanent compounds are printed as one word (solid).

Continued on next page

For general matters of spelling, *Chicago* recommends *Webster's Third New International Dictionary* and its abridgement, *Merriam-Webster's Collegiate Dictionary,* 10th edition. In some cases, the hyphen is considered part of the word.

1. Compounds with *well-, ill-, better-, best-, little-, lesser-,* etc., are hyphenated before the noun unless the expression carries a modifier. Phrases (like *how-to*) used as adjectives should be hyphenated in any position.

    The **well-known** author finally completed his **how-to** book about home gardening.

2. Because *well known* carries the modifier *very,* it isn't hyphenated. The adjective *well-intentioned* follows the verb, but it's in the dictionary with a hyphen.

    The **very well known** politician was **well-intentioned,** but he was unable to communicate effectively with his constituents.

3. In this sentence *decision making* is an object plus a present participle. In cases like this, hyphenate the object and participle before the noun. When *decision making* stands alone as a noun, rather than modifying a noun, it's two words. Hyphenate *all-* compounds whether they precede or follow the noun. The word *bookkeeping* is a permanent compound.

    The **decision-making** procedures were established after an **all-inclusive** study of the **bookkeeping** department.

4. A phrase used as an adjective, like *out-of-season,* is hyphenated in any position. A compound composed of a cardinal number plus the word *odd* is hyphenated before or after the noun. (Without a hyphen between *hundred* and *odd,* the word *odd* means "strange.")

    The **out-of-season** merchandise was offered to our **two-hundred-odd** preferred customers.

5. Hyphenate all *in-law* words. Close up a word denoting a geographical, political, or social division followed by *-wide,* unless the word is a proper noun.

    My **brother-in-law** supports the **statewide** referendum that affects the public schools.

6. Hyphenate all *self-* compounds, whether nouns or adjectives. (Words like *selfish* and *selfsame* aren't compounds.) Words that have the prefix

co- should be printed solid unless the hyphen is needed as a guide to pronunciation, as is the case here, or to distinguish between two meanings (*cooperate* and *co-operate*).

The **self-taught** computer programmer felt **self-conscious** around his **co-workers** who had received formal training.

7. If an adverb ends in *-ly*, don't hyphenate the adverb-participle combination. Compounds with the prefix *pre-* are usually printed solid unless the hyphen is needed to distinguish between two homographs (*preposition* and *pre-position*).

The **eagerly awaited** exchange of vows finally took place after a lengthy **prenuptial** ceremony.

8. The term *vice president* can be either left open or hyphenated. Words with the prefix *non-* are printed solid unless the hyphen is needed for clarity. Compounds with *ex-* (meaning "former") are hyphenated.

The **vice president** (*or* **vice-president**) of the university was **nonplussed** by the conflict between the **ex-president** and the new president.

9. Hyphenate a compound composed of a cardinal number and a unit of measurement if the compound precedes the noun. If a series of cardinal numbers precedes the unit of measurement, each number must have its own hyphen.

The contractor needs **two- by six-inch** wood strips and **ten-, twelve-, and fourteen-foot** boards to complete the addition to the building.

10. Hyphenate compounds in which the second element is a capitalized word or a numeral (*pre-1970*). Compounds with the prefix *post-* (meaning "after") are printed solid.

The history class covered information from the **pre-Roosevelt** era to the **postwar** decade.

5-8. Hyphenating Compound Words and Phrases II

1. Most compound chemical or scientific terms require no hyphen as unit modifiers; hence, **carbon dioxide emissions, sodium chloride solution.**

2. The first three terms—**pro rata, per diem, per capita**—are of Latin origin and require no hyphens; the last term isn't and usually takes a hyphen: **per-pupil expenses.** Note that all three, however, have been so thoroughly absorbed into English that they don't require italics.

3. A compound adjective consisting of an adjective and a noun usually requires a hyphen before the noun it modifies: **large-scale project, short-term loan, high-quality product, low-income neighborhood.** Authorities are divided on whether to hyphenate compounds with comparatives or superlatives; for example, the *United States Government Printing Office Style Manual (GPO)* doesn't hyphenate **lower income neighborhood** or **best loved books,** whereas most other styles do. Style guides agree that no hyphen should be used when the expression carries a modifier: **a very well built house.**

4. Authorities give contradictory advice on handling these terms. *Words Into Type* says, "a compound adjective denoting color whose first element ends in *-ish* should be hyphenated when it precedes a noun, but it need not be hyphenated when it follows the noun it modifies. When a noun is compounded with a color, or two colors are combined, they should always be hyphenated." Hence, **bluish-green sea, sky-blue truck,** and **blue-green algae.** Conversely, *The Chicago Manual of Style,* 14th edition, hyphenates only **blue-green algae** ("If the color terms are of equal importance in the compound and do not denote a blend of colors, the compound is hyphenated"). **Bluish green paint** and **coal black** are compounds in which one term modifies the other.

5. Two joined nouns of equal value require a hyphen: **secretary-treasurer, city-state, soldier-statesman.**

6. A compound modifier consisting of a cardinal number and a unit of measurement is hyphenated when it precedes the noun: hence, **20-mile hike, six-year-old child.**

7. A compound modifier consisting of an ordinal number and a noun is normally hyphenated when it precedes the noun: **fifth-floor apartment.** No hyphen is needed when the compound is capitalized: **Twentieth Century Limited.**

8. Both terms are clear without hyphens: **$20 million project, 50 percent increase.** (*GPO* says to hyphenate **50-percent increase.**)

9. **Grand jury decision, stock exchange building,** and **bubonic plague outbreak** are all clear without hyphens.

10. Almost all compound modifiers consisting of an object and a present participle are hyphenated if they precede the noun: hence, **eye-catching decor, interest-bearing account.** One exception is a well-established compound: *word processing equipment.*

11. Compound adjectives consisting of a past participle and a noun or adverb are hyphenated when they precede the noun they modify (**poverty-stricken family, hard-boiled eggs**) and often when they don't (**The eggs were hard-boiled**), unless the adverb ends in *-ly* or the term otherwise couldn't be misread: **poorly equipped kitchen.**

5-9. Hyphenating Compound Words and Phrases III

Here are the answers. Any exceptions to the rules given in the sidebar on page 208 are explained in detail. For more examples, see *The Chicago Manual of Style,* 14th edition *(Chicago).*

1. **top-secret military facility**

2. **government-sponsored cover-up**

3. **three- by five-inch cards**

4. **planned seven-day follow-up** and **stepped-up inspections**

5. **over-the-hill reporter** and **off-the-record sources**

6. **all-out battle among the 21-member executive committee**

7. **seven thousand hundred-dollar bills** (*Chicago* says, "Adjectival compounds consisting of spelled-out whole numbers are hyphenated or open following the same rules that apply to whole numbers used as nouns....Compound nouns spelling out numbers from one through ninety-nine, whether standing alone or as part of a larger number, are hyphenated. All other numbers or parts of numbers are open.")

Continued on next page

8. **third-act problems; first- and second-act problems** (In a suspended compound, such as **first- and second-act**, the hyphen marks the place of the omitted (but implied) word. If the compound has three elements, be sure to punctuate the series correctly: *four-, five-, and six-year-old children*.)

9. **stock-car-racing picture** (*The New Yorker* used hyphens, presumably treating *stock-car-racing* as a compound adjective modifying *picture*. However, both *Webster's* and *American Heritage* dictionaries omit the hyphen from *stock car*. If the first hyphen is omitted, the second one should be left off or possibly replaced with an en dash—see *Chicago*, page 188. The phrase is slightly ambiguous, however: It could mean a picture of a stock car engaged in racing or a stock photo of a racing car.)

10. **nonexclusive, five-year deal**

11. **a high-risk, high-return investment**

12. **long-sought-after top quark**

13. **high-energy physics facilities** (It's clear enough without a hyphen between *energy* and *physics*.)

14. **chintz-bedecked Louis Quatorze suite**

15. **30-minute ride in a propeller-driven airboat**

16. **two-lane Tamiami Trail**

17. **well-qualified entry-level applicants** (Because *well-qualified* modifies *entry-level applicants*, there's no comma between the two compounds.)

18. **last-chance gas station**

19. **stiff-upper-lip style**

20. **eight in-flight engine shutdowns and 16 cabin-pressure problems**

21. **30 percent fall** (According to *Chicago*, "Compounds consisting of a number followed by *percent*, which is not a unit of measure but an expression of ratio, are always open.")

22. 12-step recovery and relapse-prevention movement

23. strong behind-the-scenes role

24. 2.5-square-mile peninsula

25. a so-called open-access ruling regarding heavily polluting coal-fired plants

26. free-market economy approach (The same reasoning applies here as in number 13.)

27. oak pollen-induced rhinitis (*Chicago* would use an en dash here.)

28. long-term, low-dose anti-infective medication regimens (Many styles use a hyphen in a compound if the last letter of the prefix and the first letter of the word to which it's attached are the same.)

29. Washington-born, -bred, and -educated politician (In this case, unlike number 8, the first half of the compound is the same and the second varies. Again, watch the spacing and punctuation.)

30. often imitated, never duplicated techniques (According to *Chicago*, "Adjectival compounds consisting of adverbs not ending in -*ly* followed by participles or adjectives may be open in any position if ambiguity is unlikely.")

31. user-friendly technically advanced software

32. non-college-bound seniors (*College-bound* is contrasted with *non-college-bound*; the prefix can't be closed up or else it would mean that the students were bound to noncollege.)

33. open, sun-blasted prairies

34. macro- and microeconomics (*Chicago* says, "When alternative prefixes are offered for one word, the prefix standing alone takes a hyphen.")

5-10. Alphabetizing Index Entries

NYPL offers helpful advice:

> In all modern alphabetization systems...numbers written in numerals are sorted before letters of the alphabet, not as if they were spelled out. House styles may differ....

> Subscript and superscript numerals are filed as if they were "on-the-line" numerals preceded by a space....

> Numbers used as prefixes in the names of chemical compounds are ignored in alphabetization....

> Roman numerals should be filed in numerical order according to their arabic equivalents....Numerals in nonarabic notation are listed with their arabic equivalents....

> Dates or other numbers that form a time series are arranged chronologically....

> Abbreviations and acronyms are alphabetized as written, not as if spelled out, according to all indexing codes published since 1980. This simplifies computer sorting and is more straightforward than the old practice of listing as if spelled out....Names beginning with *Mac, Mc, Saint, St.,* or *Ste.* are alphabetized exactly as written....

> Initial articles in titles and names are often a source of confusion. Should they be omitted, inverted, or ignored? How do the rules apply to foreign languages? The answer is, "It depends." Initial articles should not be inverted or omitted, but in some cases they are ignored for purposes of alphabetization....

> Place names and personal names that include initial articles as an integral part of the name are alphabetized under the article....

> The initial articles *The, A,* and *An* as part of a title or a corporate name that does not begin with a personal name or place name are ignored in alphabetization.

Letter-by-Letter Style

Boeing passenger aircraft
   727
   737
   747
   767
Costa, Victor
cost accounting
costume design
cost-volume-profit relationship
D^3 Corporation
D Is for Dog
Edwardian era
1812 Overture
El Greco
Henry II
Henry V
Henry VIII
5-hydroxyindoleacetic acid
hypertension
The Kamber Group
Las Vegas
Louis XIV
Louis 14th furniture
Macdonald, James
MacDonald, James A.
Macleod, James A.
McDonald, James
1982 annual report
1992 annual report
Saint Joan
Saint John
St. John's
Ste.-Marie
Tankerman Manual
tank trucks
The Hague

Word-by-Word Style

1812 Overture
1982 annual report
1992 annual report
Boeing passenger aircraft
   727
   737
   747
   767
cost accounting
cost-volume-profit relationship
Costa, Victor
costume design
D^3 Corporation
D Is for Dog
Edwardian era
El Greco
Henry II
Henry V
Henry VIII
5-hydroxyindoleacetic acid
hypertension
The Kamber Group
Las Vegas
Louis XIV
Louis 14th furniture
Macdonald, James
MacDonald, James A.
Macleod, James A.
McDonald, James
Saint Joan
Saint John
St. John's
Ste.-Marie
tank trucks
Tankerman Manual
The Hague

5-11.   Catching Errors in Internet Addresses

1.   The comma would cause an e-mail program to interpret this as two separate addresses: **12345** (a local address, with no host name) and **4321@compuserve.com**, both of which are almost certainly non-existent users. The correct address is **12345.4321@compuserve.com**.

2.   All sorts of weird things are possible before the *at* sign in an e-mail address, and some people have gateways between their intraoffice e-mail system and the Internet that require cumbersome syntax. This address is legal as it is:
/s=d.louie/ou1=s56l12h@mhs-fswa.attmail.com

3.   Spaces aren't allowed in Internet addresses. E-mail systems often use underscores, periods, or dashes to separate first and last names in addresses. Query whether it should be **Lisa_Samuels@acme.com**, **Lisa.Samuels@acme.com**, **Lisa-Samuels@acme.com**, **LisaSamuels@acme.com**, or even just plain **Samuels@acme.com**.

4.   The last period should be a slash, since **eye** isn't a valid top-level domain. The correct URL is **http://www.eeicom.com/eye/**.

5.   The underscore character isn't allowed in host names. The correct URL is **http://www.the-times.co.uk**.

6.   The slash after **www** should be a period, because **www** isn't a complete host name. The correct URL is **http://www.switchboard.com**.

7.   The backslashes should be regular slashes. The correct URL is **http://www.stroud.com/new.html**.

8.   The first part is missing a *t* and a slash. Not all host names for Web sites begin with **www**. The correct URL is **http://clever.net/quinion/words/**.

 INDEX

Colophon

This book was constructed by the design and production divisions of EEI Communications in Alexandria, VA, and printed by Edwards Brothers, Inc., in Ann Arbor, MI.

Davie Smith art directed, Peter Buttecali designed the cover, and Jennifer W. Stewart designed text.

Jean Spencer word processed early drafts; Teresa Wallace and Lynn Whiteley created final pages.

The cover was produced using Adobe Illustrator 7.0 with Commander and Tasse fonts on 10 pt. C1S. Text was produced using QuarkXPress 3.32 with Commander, Helvetica, Tasse, Bembo, and Univers fonts on 60 # Arbor Smooth.